PAUL RUNYAN'S BOOK
FOR SENIOR GOLFERS

Ronald Teacher congratulates Paul Runyan as he receives the Teacher Trophy and the winner's check for the 1962 P.G.A. Seniors' Teacher Trophy Championship for the second year in a row.

PAUL RUNYAN'S BOOK FOR SENIOR GOLFERS

by PAUL RUNYAN

1961–1962 SENIOR P.G.A. CHAMPION
AND WORLD'S SENIOR CHAMPION

ILLUSTRATED

DODD, MEAD & COMPANY   NEW YORK

Copyright © 1962 by Paul Runyan
All rights reserved

No part of this book may be reproduced in any form
without permission in writing from the publisher

Printed in the United States of America

My thanks to Tom Vogt, without whose help and word
wizardry this book could not have turned out right.

PAUL RUNYAN

THE GOLFING CAREER OF PAUL RUNYAN

PAUL RUNYAN, a 54 year-old professional golfer from La Jolla, California, a national figure in golf for over a quarter of a century, is now enjoying a new reign in the spotlight as champion of the P.G.A. senior golfers, those members who have reached their fiftieth birthday.

In February 1962 in Dunedin, Florida, Runyan duplicated his feat of the year before by winning the P.G.A. Seniors' Teacher Trophy Championship. He defeated a record field of 392 entrants. Runyan has also twice travelled to Great Britain as the guest of the firm of Wm. Teacher & Sons, Ltd., co-sponsors of the senior tournament, and has twice defeated the British senior champion to capture the World's Senior Championship.

Runyan first gained golfing fame during the 1930's and the early 40's when he earned the nickname of "Little Poison." Besides taking many sectional titles, he won the P.G.A. Championship twice under match play conditions. His first victory came in 1934 and his second, probably the greatest of his career, came in 1938 when he beat a newcomer named Sam Snead, 8 and 7.

Runyan represented the United States in the Ryder Cup Matches in 1933 and 1935 and was also chosen on Ryder Cup teams in 1939 and 1941 when, however, the matches were not played because of World War II.

In recent years, Runyan has become very widely known as a teaching professional. He has given more than 40,000 golf lessons to beginners, average players and even to tournament stars like Gene Littler and Phil Rodgers.

In the four years that Runyan has been eligible for the 50 and over Senior P.G.A. event, he has carved for himself a remarkable record. In 1959 and 1960 he tied for second. Then as we have seen in 1961 and 1962 he captured both the P.G.A. Seniors' Teacher Trophy Championship and the World's Senior crown. In winning his titles, Runyan defeated such tournament stars as Jimmy Demaret, Dutch Harrison and the inimitable Gene Sarazen.

"One of the greatest things that has happened to golf in recent years is Ronald Teacher's interest and enthusiasm for the P.G.A. Seniors' Championship," said Runyan at the 1961 tournament trophy presentation. "It has given all of us golf professionals over 50, particularly those who have been club and teaching pros rather than touring pros, a second chance, a new incentive."

FOREWORD

EVERYONE knows, of course, that Paul Runyan has long been one of the finest players of the game, both as a tournament player and now in the senior class. More than this, I know that during all this period he has been a very keen student of golfing technique and a highly competent and experienced instructor. I can think of no one better qualified to write an authoritative book on golf instruction than Paul.

Robert T. Jones, Jr.

CONTENTS

THE GOLFING CAREER OF PAUL RUNYAN   v

FOREWORD BY ROBERT T. JONES, JR.   vii

1. TRAINING METHODS   1
2. THOUGHT PROCESSES   5
3. THE GRIP   9
4. THE STANCE, OR ADDRESS POSITION   20
5. THE SWING PLANE   25
6. PUTTING   29
7. CHIPPING   44
8. THE PITCH SHOTS   53
9. BUNKER SHOTS   66
10. THE MEDIUM IRONS   76
11. THE LONG IRONS   83
12. THE FAIRWAY WOODS   91
13. THE DRIVE   102
14. ODD LIES   118
15. EQUIPMENT   129
16. TOURNAMENT TIPS   145

CHAPTER 1

TRAINING METHODS

I'VE heard golfers say that as we get older we should give in gracefully to the physical limitations of age, but I believe the very opposite: that we ought to resist them with every fibre of our being. I don't mean we should knock ourselves out by more play or practice than is good for us. Yet the widespread tendency among those past forty to let nature take its course and to allow muscles and reflexes to deteriorate seems not only sad to me, but easily avoidable. True, at that stage of life the golfer cannot act as though he were twenty. He won't be able to neglect his physical conditioning for long periods of time and then, by a crushing load of work and practice, suddenly force himself back into shape again. He will have to pay regular attention to keeping himself in form.

So in my middle fifties I have found that a constant program of simple exercises has not only helped me hold my ground, but has actually enabled me to hit the ball harder than I ever did before. These exercises are not strenuous. They do not tax the heart. After doing them I do not even breathe more heavily. They are designed to affect and strengthen only those muscles in the hands and arms which are so important for accelerating the clubhead in the hitting area.

The best way to reach these particular muscles is to swing just as you do in golf, with something considerably heavier than your golf clubs. I have found an ordinary garden rake to be ideal for this purpose. Swing it out of sight somewhere, or in the dark, so your neighbors won't think you've suddenly lost your mind. The rake should be very heavy and very stiff. The stiffness makes your hands and arms do all the work of starting and stopping the rake as you move it through the normal arc of a golf swing, and its great length, with the weight so far removed, helps tire the muscles very quickly.

The average iron rake is probably fifteen or twenty times the swing weight of the average golf club. By using it for no more than two or three minutes a night just before going to bed you can prevent your hands from losing their strength and snap during long periods when you are not playing and you can also add considerably to the flexibility and quickness of the hands.

Other related exercises undoubtedly condition you over all, but do not have as much specific golfing benefit, at least for me. The rake is much better for this purpose than the weighted golf clubs often advertised. Such clubs, or the specially weighted head covers placed on conventional clubs, certainly have a useful function; they are primarily warmer-uppers, or the golf version of the two or three bats a baseball player uses just before he steps into the batting box. But they are not heavy enough to give your arms and hands the stretching and strengthening produced by a rake. Rakes are also stiffer to swing; with them, the hands and arms must do all the work, because there is no "give" to the shaft as there is with a weighted club.

This hand strengthening program can, of course, be overdone. Perhaps a lighter object, a garden hoe, or broom, should be used initially. And then when a rake is taken up it should be swung very slowly at first. If it is kept from hitting the ground at the bottom of the arc you can be sure your hands are bearing the brunt of the work. You want to tire them out as rapidly as you can. As you find your hands becoming stronger, you should swing the rake faster.

Swinging a golf shaft with no clubhead on it, or swinging some other very light object, speeds up your reflexes, too. For here we are dealing with the true power generators of the correct golf swing. Therefore, to retain our length off the tee as we get older we must keep these muscles from shortening and growing less supple through disuse. As a matter of fact, I am convinced if I'd begun this program of exercises at twenty-three instead of at forty-three, I'd be a two-hundred-and-seventy yard hitter right now. But in spite of starting them relatively late in life, I am still ten or fifteen yards longer now than I ever was.

I do not attach as much importance to conditioning the legs. But as a golf professional working the year around outdoors, I walk so much that I don't need to worry about keeping them in shape. Those of you who sit at a desk all week, and who cannot get out even on weekends during the winter, are bound to find walking itself no easy matter. In most parts of the country the electric cart is not ordinarily available either, at least on anything like the scale it is used in California or Florida. So, to keep the leg muscles from losing their tone, I recommend one very good exercise.

Lie on the floor on your back. Draw your knees up to the abdomen as far as they will go and then extend your legs full length. Point your toes, but do not let your heels touch the floor. Ten or more extensions will begin to burn the stomach muscles a bit, and the leg muscles will get a good lengthening out and stretching. Fifteen of these at first is probably the right limit. If you can raise the amount to twenty-five you are doing enough. And again this sort of exercise does not exert your whole body too strenuously. No great demand is put upon the heart.

Furthermore, the regularity of such preparation seems to help the nerves as well. A sound program of physical conditioning enables you to conquer the jitteriness likely to strike older players on and around the greens. And I'm not just talking about tournament players in the major championships either. The choking point on dollar Nassaus around the club, or even on bettering best scores, somehow seems to grow more frequent as we get older.

In this connection, I even call upon nutrition to help me. I now carry a jar of honey and a few slices of bread in the golf bag; I eat some along the way whenever I feel hungry or have butterflies in my stomach. The honey pot to be sure may raise a few false hopes in playing partners that old Runyan's gone off the wagon and is going to offer everybody a few snorts. Nevertheless, the psychological effect on me is very beneficial.

I think more lessons like these, on how to maintain power and stamina, are just waiting to be learned. Golfing longevity is being increased all the time. Today we have such players as Jerry Barber, who became P.G.A. Champion at the age of forty-five. Ben Hogan, too, won all his major titles, from the age of thirty-five to forty-five. Before thirty-five his record had been largely unimpressive. Sam Snead is, of course, still winning tournaments, and I bet he will be doing so ten years from now. Dutch Harrison after forty has been far more successful than he ever was before.

Still I don't want to give you any hogwash about never getting old. I have already said that your hands and arms must be kept active. And this can be done by exercises which do not increase the pulse rate or leave you huffing and puffing afterwards. But the trunk and spine, I suspect, present greater problems. I for one find it hard these days to stay over the ball properly throughout the swing. The willowy action of the hips which allows one to do so is gone.

I suffer a few more back and hip pains from trying to hold the head in position. Yet even these can be relieved if I chin myself on a door frame every day, letting the weight of the legs stretch the spine and vertebrae for just a few moments so that they don't jam on me and pinch.

In other words, it is not hard to keep the body in shape for a long time. If you don't think so, take a look at Gene Sarazen or Dick Metz or any number of similar stars; all of them still hit the ball vigorously. Diversity of interests, however, may scatter their concentration and competitive edge.

But the record is clear: at fifty, or sixty or even seventy years of age, you do not need to lie down and roll over, insofar as this game is concerned, unless that's really what you want to do. There's certainly no other reason for giving up golf.

CHAPTER 2

THOUGHT PROCESSES

AT the outset let me qualify the role of the right mental approach. I do not believe in working myself up on the spur of the moment by the right sort of fight talk. The psychological side of golf is very closely linked to physical conditioning and sound fundamentals. Without adequate preparation beforehand, psychological tips produce greater tension than effective combative spirit.

So the player who both keeps his body in tune and understands the dynamics of a golf swing also puts himself into a much better, more positive frame of mind. Knowing he has done a lot to help himself in advance, he is able to play with confidence. If he has not done this preliminary work, he finds himself wondering, even during a good round, when the lightning will strike. As a result it invariably strikes! Jimmy Thompson, with his powerful swing, was a good example of how lack of practice eats away the confidence of even a courageous competitor.

Nevertheless, after even the most thorough preparations we must deal with that tricky, psychological remnant. It still separates a lot of men from a lot of boys. And I must admit that if I had to choose between a player with an excellent technique, but only a fair attitude, and another with a fair technique but a superior mental approach, I would take the latter every time. For the forty years in which I have watched and participated in championship golf, I have seen countless players, past and present, in each category. Dick Grout—a competitor no longer known to many of you—could hit the ball as well as any man I ever saw. But he had such a shocking lack of mental control that he was never able to tap a fraction of his great potential.

On the other hand, less-stylish players like Walter Hagen, Johnny Revolta, Billy Casper, Doug Ford, or Doug Sanders get an almost indecent amount of mileage—simply because of their outstanding psychological resourcefulness. What is their secret?

Positive thinking comes first, but this is more than a trite phrase, and not as simple as it sounds. For example, if you are facing a shot to a green guarded by a deep trap to the left, what mental directives do you give yourself? If you say, "Don't hit to the left," you will probably push the shot much too far to the right. Or, having decided to give the trap a wide berth, you might at the last moment, doubt even your negative approach, and tell yourself, "For heaven's sake don't over-correct." So you end up in the bunker anyway! However in neither of these cases have you thought about where you *are* trying to hit the ball. You have not thought positively.

I am indebted to Olin Dutra for this psychological tip. He says that in every tournament he ever won he was only conscious of what he was trying *to* do, and never of what he was trying *not* to do.

But now I would like to carry this advice one step farther and urge you to give exclusive attention not only to what you're trying *to* do, but also to what *you're* trying to do. When I catch myself watching an opponent or being concerned with his performance my own game invariably suffers. This is especially true when you're nervous. You must then tell yourself that the other fellow is just as keyed up as you are, if not more so, and go about your own business exclusively.

In my good tournaments—and especially in my best seventy-two hole performance, a 273 at the Charleston, South Carolina Waupoo links in 1935, I remember being under the very real and pleasant illusion that I was the only player on the course. Unfortunately I don't know how to bring about this illusion time after time. I'm only saying that it's a great aid to good golf when it does occur. Far more frequently we enjoy this affirmative trance only while things are going well. Then we explode at the first stroke of bad luck and by the time the round is over we feel very very sorry for ourselves indeed. I've gone bumping down these mental steps more often than I like to remember.

This brings me to my third point: that anybody, even the best striker of the ball who ever lived, is going to make his share of mistakes. The average golfer is sure to mis-hit to some degree ninety to ninety-five percent of his shots. The average tournament expert may reduce this percentage but it is amazing how many shots even he misses. Thus your reaction to this chronic imperfection determines your actual skill. Don't let the bad shots get to you. Don't let yourself become angry. For the true scramblers are thick-skinned. They follow their bad shots with no dramatics, and redeem their mistakes by good recoveries. They do not pose. And they always beat the whiners.

Such mental control does not come easy to me, either. But when I am most successful I am always cool and collected.

Here I am past the half-century mark and I have to tell myself firmly again and again to walk slowly instead of charging after the ball, to relax if things go badly, instead of fussing and fuming, and generally to pace all my actions so that a jerky rush and hurry doesn't creep into my swing—or, to put it positively, to be sure that I swing with the proper rhythm.

Dutch Harrison is a prime example of a player who gears himself to this smooth pace of playing and moving. But he does this so naturally I doubt that he even has to think about it. As a result, he has not only retained an effortless-looking rhythm but beats all the youngbloods in the field even during the final thirty-six holes of major events.

This refusal to get worked up over poor shots—or, at any rate, the ability to absorb them, retrieve them, and go on as though they never happened—can make up for many technical shortcomings.

8 THOUGHT PROCESSES

My last point, closely connected to these others, is that you should never give up, no matter how black your chances look. And by the same token, no lead should ever be considered safe. Take for example, the famous match between Al Watrous and Bobby Cruikshank in the 1932 P.G.A. Watrous was eleven up with thirteen to play. He then conceded a five-foot putt. If Bobby had missed it he would have been twelve down with twelve to play, but even with this gift, Cruikshank stood eleven down with twelve to go.

Poor Al Watrous! On those next twelve holes he made eight pars, three bogeys, and one birdie, but he lost them all except for the eighteenth hole where his birdie gave him a tie. Then after seven extra holes he finally lost in a sudden death play-off.

Believe me, you never know what is going to happen in golf. If you ever quit before you find out you just haven't played the game for all it's worth.

CHAPTER 3

THE GRIP

HANDS adhering to the club shaft correctly and getting the right feel are indispensable to good shots. It's like the nursery tale of the woman getting home with her pig. "Stick won't beat dog, dog won't bite pig, pig won't jump fence, and I can't get home tonight." For if the grip isn't right, nothing else will be either. Everything that follows in the swing itself will have to compensate for faulty hand position. And, like the poor old woman, you won't get home either.

Of course, there has always been controversy as to what does constitute the right position, and this is still true. The subject has been discussed in every golf book ever written. And yet we must cover it again here. For it will be worth while if we can add just one or two small details to all that has been said before, or clarify one or two old points.

To begin with, when you take hold of the club with the left hand the shaft should lie obliquely across the palm, with the bell-shaped end tucked firmly under the heel of the hand. (Fig. 1). The shaft is then running through the bottom joint of the middle finger to the middle joint of the first finger. (Fig. 2). The back of the left hand should then be turned over the shaft so that when you look down you see three knuckles. The inverted "V" formed by closing your thumb and index finger should point to your right shoulder. (Fig. 3). The "V" must always be kept closed or squeezed

10 THE GRIP

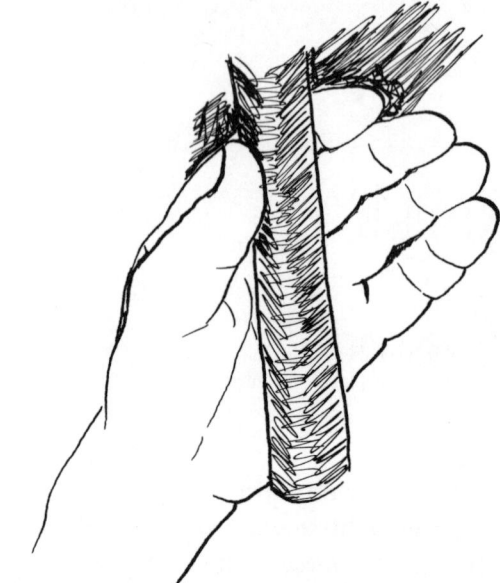

FIG. 1

FIG. 2

THE GRIP 11

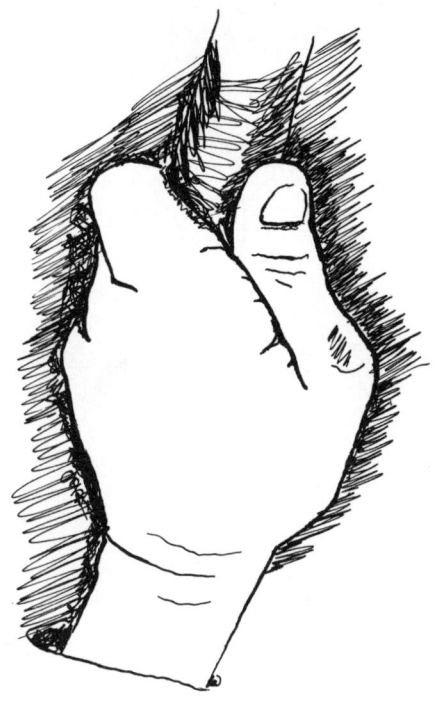

FIG. 3

together down to the joint of the thumb. This sort of closed "V" is referred to as the short thumb position. If the "V" is entirely open so that the club slides down into it, your swing will be too loose. One of the major beneficial changes in Ben Hogan's grip, between his also-ran and his championship days, was from this long thumb to the short thumb position.

The left hand, now, turned to where you see three knuckles, has put the club into a position of purchase. Under the stress of pivoting it can do its share of getting the clubhead through correctly. Pressure is mainly in the last three fingers, although the thumb itself acts as a kind of set-screw against which the fingers can hold the shaft in place.

Now with the face of the club directionally at right angles to the line of flight the right hand is put on as though it were shaking hands, with the palm exactly parallel to the directional posi-

12 THE GRIP

FIG. 4

tion of the club face—or exactly at right angles to the line of flight. (Fig. 4). Another check is to have the inverted "V" of the right hand, which is also kept pinched or closed, pointing straight up at your nose.

The shaft is held entirely in the fingers of the right hand, and runs from the bottom joint of the third finger to the middle joint of the index finger, more square and less oblique than it does in the left hand. The right little finger—with certain exceptions that we'll get to later—normally laps over the left index finger. (Fig. 5).

The left thumb is now contained in the right palm, in the natural cleft caused by bringing the right hand up to what I term a natural position. I'm aware of contributing my bit of prejudice here, for many teachers say this "V" should also point to the right shoulder. But in my opinion the right hand can "trigger" the clubhead action in the hitting area (as Tommy Armour says) far more powerfully from this position.

FIG. 5

14 THE GRIP

It is tremendously important to grip the club in this consistent manner. Only when you've done it consistently well can you ever hope to combine power and control and set your timing up properly. For if you change the relation of your hands at address you necessarily alter the action you must perform to hit the ball.

I object to the right hand "V" pointing at the right shoulder because it takes away the trigger action most of us need in the hitting area. And when a player is using such a grip, the clubhead must be pulled through the ball more stiffly to avoid a snap hook. For big, young fellows with power to spare, this method often works well, I admit. They can hit the ball far enough simply with a stiff-armed action, like a forehand in tennis.

But those of us who need the wrist snap to develop adequate distance had better put the right hand in the position I advocate, where its full throw or trigger can be delivered without closing the face too much. Especially later in your life this becomes important, because stiff push shots then begin to exert overly severe demands on your hip and back. For proof of this look at the physical troubles many players of this school run into in their thirties and forties.

To repeat—if your hands grip the club inconsistently your timing must be inconsistent also if you are to hit your shots straight. The more I turn my hands back, with both "V's" pointing to the right, the less I can use my wrists coming into the ball.

Conversely, if I point the left hand "V" at my nose and the right hand "V" at my left shoulder (the weakest and poorest grip I can think of), the thrust or flip of the wrists would have to become too exaggerated, and the arm and body action would have to stop almost entirely for the ball to go straight. Plainly this grip wouldn't allow me to hit the ball anywhere either.

So get the hands properly on the club. With a semi-palm, semi-finger grip, turn the left hand back until you see three knuckles (and if you insist on experimenting, do your experimenting here, on a limited scale, to find precisely how strong the left hand should be carried). Then grip the club completely in the fingers of the right hand, or throwing hand, with this right "V" pointing

THE GRIP

at the nose. (Again, if you want to split hairs, I'll settle for the right eye, but no farther right than that.)

The great players have always demonstrated the year-in and year-out effects of a sound grip. Because they are careful to put their hands correctly on the club they play consistently good golf with a minimum of strain and effort. Number one in this group, in my opinion, because of the artistic look of his long slender hands and fingers, is Tommy Armour. For the thirty years I have watched him his grip has never varied from perfection. Others with equally sound hand positions still cannot match the grace with which he holds a club.

Arnold Palmer's grip is also excellent. In the last four years, I believe, his game improved mainly because of his improved grip. I've heard people say that Palmer points both 'V's' over his right shoulder. Maybe he did a couple of years ago, but he certainly doesn't now.

In my own case, I believe I've always had a good grip. Once in my search for power, I tried the ten-fingered or "baseball" grip and found it had exactly the opposite effect. I was straighter, but shorter. If people with sufficiently broad hands put all their fingers on the club, they seem to end up just pushing the ball. The Vardon overlapping grip normally gives them more of a whipping action. At any rate, I for one decided that I couldn't afford the five or ten yards this experiment cost me.

My only other variation (and this was unintentional) has been a tendency to let the left hand get too weak at times, with two, instead of three, knuckles showing. Then to keep from hitting the ball to the right, I have to cast the club too soon, or too much from the top of the swing. Some of our very best players, such as Gene Littler, unconsciously allow their grips to change from time to time. Occasionally he used to raise his hands; this forced the V's to separate, the right hand to go back a few degrees, and the left to go forward. Phil Rodgers, too, one of our brightest new stars, occasionally slips into this habit.

Dow Finsterwald, on the other hand, has had an excellent grip every time I've seen him. Sam Snead also has held the club well

16   THE GRIP

FIG. 6

over an unusually long period of time; he never seems to change one iota. And Bobby Jones was another great golfer whose grip suggested the strong, delicate hands of a surgeon.

Gene Sarazen uses a marked variation of the standard grip described above. The casual observer, looking at Gene's hands on the club, would say they approximate the positions I recommend. But with his stubby hands and short fingers he found that he could get more flexibility by placing his left thumb, not on the club shaft as in the Vardon overlapping grip I have just described (which probably ninety-five percent of our best players use), but outside the right hand completely, tucked in behind the heel. He then interlocks the index finger of the left hand with the little finger of the right. (Fig. 6). Lloyd Mangrum and Claude Harmon are other exponents of this grip. It is the only sort of interlocking grip I ever recommended, but it still is not one of my favorites. In my earlier teaching days I experimented along these lines, and usually the result, in spite of sometimes adding power, was too much loss of control.

THE GRIP 17

A better variant of the Vardon overlapping, even if it does not work for me, is the so-called baseball grip, where all the fingers are on the shaft of the club, with no interlocking or overlapping. (Fig. 7). Actually it has nothing to do with baseball. The left thumb is still inside the right palm. More than that, the club shaft is still held over fifty percent in the fingers, not entirely in the palms as a batter holds a bat. (Sometimes I have wondered why placement hitters in baseball do not experiment with a golf grip to see if it works.)

This eight (or, counting the thumbs, ten) fingered grip does seem to help many people, women especially, or those with long slender fingers and hands too narrow to cover enough space on the shaft to give firmness to the swing. Art Wall has used it with great success. It firmed up his backswing that had been a bit too floppy because his narrow hands bunched together in the Vardon overlapping grip. Dai Rees, from England, is another advocate of this grip, as is our own Bob Rosburg.

This discussion of how to hold the club now leads us to the subject of different textures of club grips. You must discover by trial and error just what suits your type of skin in various weather conditions. The prospect of rain, for instance, used to make me feel anxious for a whole round, until I hit upon the idea of carrying friction tape with me and twisting it in spirals onto the shafts of my clubs if the going got wet. After that I didn't even have to keep my hands dry to hold on adequately and get plenty of power in my shots. Furthermore, I could stop looking at the sky and attend to my game.

Aside from the elements, some of us have skins either too dry or too moist for certain kinds of grips. Dry skin, for example, does not go well with leather grips except in the hottest weather. Rubberized grips are much better for such hands. Conversely, if your skin tends to be too moist or oily, the Burke Park all-weather grip is preferable. It is made of rubber and cotton cord. Yet, this kind of grip, though ideally suited to wet weather, must be artificially moistened if you hope to hang onto your club in an extremely dry climate like that in the desert.

18   THE GRIP

FIG. 7

Continuous play in a warm climate generally favors leather. But during the cold months this material becomes much too hard and slick to hold. A mixture of glycerine and rose water on the hands—which football players also use against the cold—helps bring out the skin's natural oils. Beeswax in various commercial preparations is a bit less effective, I find, but better than nothing.

Grip thickness is equally important for a firm, but not tense hold on the club. If your hands are small and weak, you need large grips to keep you from feeling that you are simply holding the shaft in your fists. However, such a big grip should taper sharply, so that your hands can develop a slinging, rather than a pushing action. Long-fingered people also need big grips so they won't gouge themselves with their finger nails. Only very strong and very small-handed players should ever use very small grips.

Now if you feel I have spent too much time discussing the various kinds of grips, just watch the care with which a great player takes hold of his club. Once, back in Hot Springs, when I was an apprentice in club-making, the great MacDonald Smith asked me to put on some grips for him. He gave explicit orders. I was not to use any glue at all beneath the listing, a light-weight sort of padding underneath the leather itself. He would not blame me, he said, if the grips proved too loose, or even came off in his hands. But under no circumstances was I to add any glue to make the listing adhere.

I nodded and started the job at once. But it seemed wasteful to risk ruining all my work by letting these grips slide off, especially since the tiniest bit of glue here and there might hold them. I was careful, I thought, to use very, very little glue, figuring that beneath the listing and calfskin nobody could possibly detect it. Nevertheless, when Mac Smith came in the shop next morning and wrapped those sensitive hands around the first club I had fixed he looked at me dourly and insisted I do them all over again. I went back to work a little wiser.

CHAPTER 4

THE STANCE, OR ADDRESS POSITION

WHILE it is difficult to say too much about the grip and its vital influence on everything in the swing, I have often heard too much importance attributed to the stance. The usual mistake is to blame either hooking or slicing on whether a line across the toes points to the right or left of the target. The first is called a closed stance. The second an open stance. But this imaginary line really governs only the direction in which the ball *starts*. Of course, this direction is not always *at* the hole. And in the power shots, when you wish to deliver the fullest possible hit from the fullest possible turn, you aim this line down the right side of the fairway, so that a slight right to left flight and roll of the ball (hook) will bring you back into the middle. Conversely, with a pin well to the right of the green, guarded by a trap, you would aim ten or fifteen yards to the left and try to cut or fade the ball slightly from left to right.

In neither case, however, does your stance determine the drift of the ball. If you are a chronic slicer, whose shots usually start toward the left rough and fade back into the fairway, and whose feet, therefore, are pointing well to the left of where the ball actually ends up, you'll feel cheated if you suddenly adopt a closed stance to help you hook. The ball will merely *start* to the right, instead of to the left, and continue its customary rainbow farther to the right, probably off the golf course altogether. Your lack of

THE STANCE, OR ADDRESS POSITION

hand action in the hitting area causes you to slice, and until you correct that deficiency you are better off aiming to the left. The predictable error will at least leave you in play.

Similarly, the inveterate hooker who opens his stance and uses the same strong thrust of his wrists will only get a left-to-left snap that will put him in the left-hand rough.

Accordingly, a change of stance will not correct either a slice or a hook. Closing up (or drawing the right foot back farther from the ball) so that a line across the toes would point to the right of the target does give you more time to get to the ball in your downswing, and thus allows your hands more time to make the clubhead catch up. By the same token, an open stance, with the right foot closer to the ball, allows you to get to it more quickly and gives the hands less time to hit. Even so, in each of these cases, it is still the *hand action* that makes the ball spin one way or the other, *not the stance,* and I think it's important to emphasize this fact.

However, if the stance only sets up the line of flight on which you *start* the ball, its effect upon trajectory is absolute. From the drive down to the nine iron or wedge each shot travels through a different flight pattern—the drive descending most gradually, and the nine iron most steeply. And each of these different trajectories is determined by the stance itself, or the address position.

The decisive element is where you place the ball in relation to the feet and to the head. Starting with the driver, the ball is played opposite the left heel. The feet as a general rule are spread to about the width of the shoulders, though obviously, like all general rules, exceptions must be made. The stance of the tall, narrow-shouldered person will be wider than his shoulders, that of the short broad-shouldered person narrower. I have seen Bobby Jones hit full practice drives with his heels practically touching; he did this both to facilitate his turn and to make himself stay put over the ball.

Actually to arrive at your own proper stance, you merely need to use a little common sense. If the muscles on the inside of your legs tighten up at address your stance is too wide. You will either

22 THE STANCE, OR ADDRESS POSITION

not turn properly (an important matter which we'll discuss later), or you will sway off the ball in trying to turn. On the other hand, if you lose your balance while pivoting your stance is obviously too narrow.

Now your head, which is the center of your swing and therefore determines the bottom of its arc, is held behind the ball for the drive, with the weight more equally distributed than for any other shot. The ball is actually struck on the upswing. Because the ball is on a tee, you can do this easily enough without hitting the ground. By controlling the ball's trajectory you minimize backspin and maximize roll.

For the fairway woods you must make a slight, but indispensable, adjustment of your address position. You move the ball back about half an inch inside the left heel. Your head comes forward exactly opposite the ball, instead of behind it as for the drive. The fairway woods should be hit precisely at the bottom of the arc, neither before the bottom for any pinching action such as you desire with the irons, nor after the bottom on the upswing as you hit the drive. This sort of sweeping action at the very bottom of the arc is properly called a lob and can be performed with any iron club as well, if on a given shot you want to get the ball up more quickly or have it roll farther than usual when it comes down. The trajectory of the normal fairway wood, because it is played closed to the center of the stance, shows a more gradual ascent and a steeper descent than the drive.

For the long irons the identical process is carried out. The ball is moved back a half inch more inside the left heel and the head is slightly in front of it now, so that you get a trace of pinching action, or backspin, to the shot, which starts up less steeply and comes down more abruptly. With the medium irons the head goes still farther in front of the ball. And for the most-lofted irons, where the pinching action can be most pronounced but the flight of the ball adequately high, the head is farthest in front of the ball. It is then struck with the steepest downswing.

So, if we say that for the drive our stance is normally fifteen inches wide, and that for the nine iron the ball is played in the

THE STANCE, OR ADDRESS POSITION 23

very middle of the stance, equi-distant from each foot, we have clearly moved the ball back approximately a half inch for each of the other thirteen clubs we use. Correspondingly, for each of those clubs the head has come farther forward. If maximum stopping action is desired, the head has to be farthest forward—which, of course, forces the weight onto the left foot. If maximum roll is desired—as with the teed-up drive—the head is actually back of the ball.

Of course, just as we discussed adaptations which different people might make in their grips, so individual stance variations are not only possble, but sometimes even desirable.

Turning the toes, especially the right toe, in or out, directly affects your pivot. If the right toe is turned in, you had better be very flexible of body, or you won't be able to turn your right hip freely enough on the backswing to hit from the inside out. If you are stiff-trunked, you'll turn much better if you toe that right foot out a little.

On the other hand, tall, loose-jointed people (tall women especially, like the very best of them all, Mickey Wright) often have a tendency to turn too far. A pigeon-toed, or knock-kneed stance helps them acquire stability, and they are still limber enough to turn adequately.

Finally, just as we mentioned that your hands had to adhere properly to the club shaft if you were to have any feel of the shots, so we should say something now about your feet fastening themselves to the ground. In my early days, when I used a rather extreme sway in order to get more leverage, I attached an extension spike to the left shoe to keep from losing all grip with that foot as it came onto the toe during the backswing. Even now, when I stay in place better, I favor an extension spike.

You should change your regular spikes, too, more often than you probably do. If you have something more substantial than stubs on the bottom of your shoes, you'll get the solid feeling necessary for a really full turn. The stress of the spikes holding, so that you actually have to turn against them, is a guarantee that you won't slip. Without such a feeling, you are not likely to trust yourself to turn fully: you will be afraid of not getting back to the ball solidly.

For this reason corrugated soles do not work for me. In dry weather the rubber-ribbed shoes are not too bad, although even then I notice they cost me six or seven yards through lack of anchor. And in wet weather I can barely stand up in them, let alone knock a golf ball very far. So pay attention to your footwear and make sure that your feet don't slip and slide around as you swing.

Now your grounding in the general fundamentals is almost complete. You know how to supervise wisely limited, but critical, physical conditioning. You've developed a valuable auxiliary in the right, helpful mental attitude. You take hold of the club soundly and consistently, and you are fully conscious of the range of stances, or address positions, to accomplish the whole range of trajectories, each with its specific effect upon roll, or lack of roll. Now we should talk about what everybody calls "the groove," and try to get you into it, before we take up the individual shots.

CHAPTER 5

THE SWING PLANE

WITH the swing plane we come to what Hogan calls the "muscle-memory" part of golf. This involves a person's ability to bring the clubhead back against the ball consistently and squarely, to hit it "on the screws" every time, without any great conscious deliberation. Doing exactly the same thing over and over is the object here, and to achieve it a player sets up his swing path, plane, or groove, so that each swing does not result in a renewed attempt to find the ball.

To visualize such a swing plane, *picture a wheel*. The wheel's radius is an imaginary line running from the top end of the spine out to the ball. Thus the outer rim of the wheel is the *clubhead*. The hands and arms are like wire *spokes* which turn this rim. The *axle* is the spine itself. The head is the *hub*.

The wheel is tipped to different angles for different clubs. Its flattest plane of rotation is about 45° for the longest club, the driver. Its steepest plane is about sixty degrees for the nine iron or wedge. The wedge is, of course, the shortest club in your bag. So when you use it you have to bring the ball closest to your feet. But you do not stand in the same posture as for a drive and simply swing your hands higher. Instead, you tip the spine forward to set up the same sort of rotating action of the wheel.

Since the hub of this wheel is the head, it must center all motion. If the hub is moving up or down while the wheel turns, much of the freedom and acceleration produced by a good swing plane is wasted. For this reason the motion pictures of my own swing used to scare the daylights out of me as an instructor, until I gave up my intentional lateral sway and decided to get the necessary extra leverage by strengthening my muscles.

Of course, our wheel illustration obscures one major reality. Nobody, after all, can bring the clubhead down on exactly the same path it followed going up. Nor, for that matter, should he. A swing such as Sam Snead's, or Gene Littler's, probably comes closest to retracing the same path. But some sort of loop (either from the outside in, as in Hogan's case, or from well inside to slightly less inside, as that of Bobby Jones) is even preferable if there is to be continuous rhythmic motion. Otherwise; the player would have to come to a complete stop at the top of his swing, before starting back down again.

Furthermore, a particular swing plane is not something a player just happens upon, or even chooses. It is first of all conditioned by his build. If he is tall and thin he can swing on a more upright plane and still have his arms and hands clear his body. The shorter, thick-chested or heavy-armed person, swinging on such a plane, would collide with himself, restricting the speed at which he could move the clubhead and probably bouncing it off himself outside the ball—producing a good case of shanks. Thus, such a player must flatten out his plane to give himself more freedom.

As a matter of fact, unusually stocky players, like Bobby Cruikshank, solve this problem by using slightly longer clubs, giving themselves more room in which to get to the ball, and actually widening their arc for more power. Cruikshank, and Sarazen, too, have used longer clubs bored to lie flatter than the conventional forty-two or forty-two-and-a-half inch driver, but neither used one longer than forty-four inches. Chick Evans' experiment with a forty-six or forty-seven-inch club strikes me as a freakish way of combating loss of distance and flexibility.

It is true that we are likely to get stouter and flabbier as we get older, so that these clubs seem the solution to physical changes. But I believe the conditioning we talked about earlier is a far sounder remedy for atrophying muscles.

One noble experiment to simplify the complications of a swing plane was conducted by Alfred Sargent at the East Lake Club in Atlanta, Georgia. He wanted to make sure that after a pupil once found his own correct plane he could always keep it, without having to tilt the wheel, as we have said, from shot to shot. Sargent simply reduced the pupil's wood clubs to the length and lie of the irons, so that this tipping of the plane was eliminated and all clubs were swung through the same arc. By this method an unusually large number of high handicap members, I am told, soon became medium handicappers. But, alas, with this solution the power element is missing. People prefer to make their mistakes at least vigorous and forceful ones, and I am inclined to agree with them.

A bad grip makes the proper swing plane harder to set up. If your hands go on the club in too strong a position, for example, with the "V's" pointing too far to the right, you will swing the club too flat. Or, if you take too weak a grip, with the "V's" pointing too far to the left, you will swing too upright.

Do not confuse these terms directionally. If you stand at right angles to a player who is planning to slice deliberately his swing plane should seem the same. He is aiming to the left, of course, so that viewed from a ninety-degree angle to what would be his straight line of flight he is taking the club back much less inside the ball than he normally does. He accomplishes this by adjusting his stance, by moving his right foot forward and his left foot back, not by swinging his hands higher. And the slice will be imparted in the hitting area when his hands intentionally fail to close the clubface.

Conversely, if he wishes to hook, he closes his stance and uses his hands strongly. From the same ninety-degree angle to what would be a straight line of flight, this swing appears flatter. But if the player performs these stance adjustments properly, and the adjustments in hand action that accompany them, his swing plane will never vary.

This is the most subtle part of a golf swing, actually, because a consistent swing plane is so hard to measure. Variations can creep in unnoticed. Historically speaking, it is not Jones or Sarazen, Snead or Hogan, Littler or Palmer who stand out in my mind as having best mastered the swing plane. It is Willie MacFarlane, a tall wisp of a man, who looked more like a professor than an athlete. Willie grooved his swing so well that his idea of a good rousing workout was to stand on the first tee before starting his round and just make four or five passes in the air with his driver to loosen himself up. The last pass might even be a bit vigorous. Then, he would hit the ball down the fairway straight as a string and go on like that throughout the entire round. MacFarlane was also sound in all the important fundamentals of grip and stance, of course. But his pipeline, monotonous straightness was mostly a product of his unvarying, effortlessly repeated swing plane. Standing about six foot-three, he swung the club quite uprightly for even that height. Willie was content to hit the ball a bit shorter than you might expect considering that he could manage a very wide arc. But if he was able to reach a green he would nearly always be *on* it. When he did miss one to the right or left, his error seemed to be primarily in his aim. In flight the ball rarely curved off line.

I've played with other golfers deservedly famous for their straightness—men like Harry Cooper or Mac Smith, to name just two—without really being overawed. If anything, I felt I was even straighter myself. But Willie MacFarlane always made me feel like a wild man. By comparison, I seemed to be zigging and zagging all over the course. And the reason for his amazing consistency was that he had *grooved* this *rotating wheel,* this swing plane, as well as any man I ever saw. He could always reproduce it and it never wobbled on him or left its track. All of us other mortals—the experts included—have days when that ball simply cannot be hit solidly. We call it bad timing or an off day, but if this happens suddenly and inexplicably and produces a little panic, our trouble more than likely lies in this swing plane getting slightly out of kilter without our knowing or even feeling it. At any rate, in such cases that is the first place to look for the trouble.

CHAPTER 6

PUTTING

IN most golf instruction books the long shots are taken up first, but I feel the reverse order considerably shortens the learning process. Grasping the principles which govern the finesse shots—putting, chipping, pitching, and bunker work—helps you to understand other shots as well. And in the all-important matter of scoring these finesse shots are always immediately decisive.

By itself, in theory, putting consumes half the strokes taken on any par seventy-two course, and more than half where par is less. Actually, on a given round of even our greatest players, this theory of thirty-six field shots bracketed with thirty-six putts is almost never borne out. Old Man Par, though no longer good enough, still beats the best best players from tee to green. It is on the greens that we must lick him. The Hogans, Nelsons, Sneads, Littlers and Palmers, hitting fifteen or sixteen greens, including some par fives in two, still have to improve upon two putts a green to win anything these days. Others with less talent, hitting twelve or thirteen greens a round, must be even better with the putter, to have any chance at all.

However, there is an equalizing factor. The player who does not strike the ball too well from tee to green has—or at least should have—a putting edge to begin with. For he will be reaching the greens with wedge or nine iron third shots, as opposed to his opponent's long iron seconds. And there is some wear and tear on the better hitter of the ball here. He feels he should be holing just as many putts, even though his are bound to be longer. Byron Nelson in particular seemed to be frustrated whenever he took more putts than the good scrambler.

Putting definitely is the fighter's one chance to match an opponent superior to him in other departments. For men of any age lacking power or control, for all women, and for ninety-nine percent of the rest of us, it is our greatest opportunity to catch up. The best golfer who ever lived, or will ever live, cannot beat par from tee to green on a lifetime basis. But any of us can beat it on the greens, if we apply ourselves. So let's get at it.

At the outset let me register a firm dissent to a statement often made by professionals themselves. They say that in this department of play more personal idiosyncracies and whims are allowable. But the notion that on these crucial pay-off shots peculiarities of style do not matter seems to me to invite trouble. I admit that in putting, as in every other part of the game, technical faults can be offset, sometimes to a remarkable extent, by superior touch, or hard work, or both, so that the player learns to time his errors.

But these faults in themselves are never helpful. The man who does his best to minimize them by grounding himself in the fundamentals simply gives his natural ability that greater chance to be effective.

Actually putting can be taught more mathematically, with less concession to personal variations, than any other part of the game. For example, if a polished player comes to me for putting instructions, I don't bother to see him in action before beginning my advice. With the fuller shots, however, I would ask him to strike the ball first.

The fact that no two great stars look alike in putting, and that none of them adopt all the features I recommend, is no rebuttal either. Billy Casper, for example, has a good style in one respect, a not-so-good one in another, and is generally a fine putter because of his positive mental approach. He stands up to the ball perfectly. He grips the club not quite so perfectly, and thus also swings it not quite perfectly. I feel, therefore, that if he ever begins to doubt himself he will not be the fine putter which somebody with sounder fundamentals like Horton Smith remained all his life. Johnny Revolta, too, although somewhat hindered on very long putts by a placement of his right foot which restricted his backswing, is a good example of how a sound grip and style lasts a lifetime. Among modern-day players—none of whom in my opinion can yet match Horton Smith—Jerry Barber demonstrates the durability of good style. He uses more wrist action than I advocate, but his method is just as sound as the dollars he has won with it.

To begin with, then, the hands should go on the club with the palms as nearly horizontal as they can be placed without locking the elbows too uncomfortably against the sides (Fig. 8). The inverted "V" of the thumb and index finger of the left hand points below the left shoulder, while the "V" of the right hand points an equal distance below the right shoulder. Another good way of checking these balanced positions is to see that each "V" points at its respective elbow.

The reason for this exaggerated supination of each hand is to lock the club in place, so that without conscious manipulation or supervision in the swing itself the face of the club neither opens nor closes. The right hand cannot pronate, or close, the face in striking the ball. The position of the left hand blocks such action by having already turned to the left as far as it will naturally go. By the same token, the left hand cannot open the face on the backswing, because of the right hand's supination. (The different grip for the full swing, or power shots, of course, is designed to do just the opposite: to release full wrist action, rather than block it. But on the greens, and for the chips, we face no such power demands.)

The player who uses this putting grip has gone a long way toward holding the club in a fixed position throughout the stroke. He is therefore able to concentrate wholly on where to aim, how to set up his stance, and what force to use in the stroke itself.

32 PUTTING

FIG. 8

Now lining up the ball assumes the greatest importance; the tiniest margin of error is enough to cause a miss. So again we must give our eyes the best possible chance to see this line correctly and to adjust the address position accordingly. From an optical standpoint it is best to have the toes exactly parallel to the line on which we want the ball to start. (Fig. 9). Johnny Revolta, whose feet were in an open stance, nevertheless acquired this squareness by bending his left knee prominently forward, which brought his hips and shoulders parallel to the line. Personally, I think its' simpler to have the whole body square to the line to begin with.

At any rate, after setting yourself up as nearly square to the line as possible, you should practically *sit down* to the ball, or bend over it in a *semi-sitting* position. Your eyes are then directly over the desired line of roll, which is also the line on which the putter should be swung back and through. (Fig. 10). Here again is the function of the square stance: to keep the eye from crossing this line.

With your weight evenly balanced, the center of the ball should be just opposite the inside of your left shoe. Be precise about this placement. If you put the ball opposite the toe one time, and inside the foot an inch or so the next, you make the hands go through too many different adjustments. Take care to standardize these alignments. They will seem unnatural only at first and will go a long way toward developing a reliable, near-automatic stroke which you can trust, and which does not have to be thought out for every single putt.

In order to take the wrists out of the stroke without undue stiffening, your grip pressure should be equalized on the putts. The right hand increases its otherwise looser hold until it grips with the same pressure as the left. This moves the actual feel of putting up into the forearms, to let them take charge, so that only the inertia of the clubhead causes the wrists to break at all. The player trying this method for the first time may find that it seems stiff and strange. But if he persists he'll be surprised and gratified at how quickly he picks up the proper rhythm and feel. For tak-

34 PUTTING

FIG. 9

FIG. 10

ing the flip out of the stroke is the best cure for the yips that I know of, and a better guarantee of striking the ball solidly every time. The major motion, therefore, comes in the *arms and shoulders*, not in the wrists or elbows. (Fig. 11).

But your arms, bent at address, must not be allowed to straighten out during the stroke, or you will stub the ground behind the ball. They must not increase their bend either, or you will top it.

There are, additionally, other factors in the grip which we should discuss. The reverse overlap is used in putting by an overwhelming majority of players today. The left index finger overlaps the right little finger, reversing the normal Vardon grip used for the other shots. However, since in putting we are trying to eliminate any slinging or flipping action of the wrists, I do not care what kind of overlap is used, or if any at all is used. As far as I'm concerned, if the hands are placed in the correctly supinated position, and if the stroke is kept in the *forearms*, the regular overlapping or even the eight-fingered grip will work just as well. I myself have gone from the conventional overlap to the reverse overlap without affecting my performance one way or the other. With a wristy putting stroke, however, the matter might assume more importance.

A more personal variation of my own concerns the right thumb. From the time I first saw Johnny Farrell curl his right thumb up as though he were shooting a marble and dig the nail into the side of the shaft, I have used such a position myself. I found that it gave a firmer, tack-hammer feel to my stroke, and eliminated any looseness or scrape. I was further convinced that it was a sound innovation when Farrell himself abandoned it and stopped putting so well. But again, I place no unusual significance on this device. If you can keep your stroke sufficiently firm without resorting to this complication, by all means don't bother with it.

The length and tempo of the stroke in putting, for all the different lengths of putts, brings us to the subtleties of distance-perception and reflexes. I myself feel that a stroke for any putt should be just long enough to get the ball to the hole (or slightly past the hole when you are inside fifteen feet on the level) with-

FIG. 11

out having to jab at the ball. If the backswing becomes too long the stroke must necessarily be softened coming through in order to stop the ball from going too far. Such deceleration takes away the tap which gives a putt its firmness.

Thus, generally speaking, the more sweeping, pendulum stroke of former days (best exemplified by Bobby Jones) which for all its delicacy was at the mercy of bumpy or grainy greens, has been replaced by a firmer, more compact hit not affected as greatly by various textures of green. By and large, the touch putters of my day have largely disappeared. They were accomplished enough on long approach putts, but from five and six feet today's tappers are much more accurate. Watch Casper, Rosburg, or Sanders, and you will see them hit, rather than sweep, the ball. (Of course, these are matters of shading. A tap can be over-shortened or hurried into a jab. And if you take the wrists out of the stroke too grimly you can stiffen up too much. Any good point can be overdone.)

In deciding how far to pass the hole, or whether to lag the putt to die right at the hole, you face another choice. I have said that fifteen feet on the level is about the outside limit of any never-up-never-in thoughts for me. Downhill the distance is less; a putt hit too firmly can leave you farther away than when you started. Thus I would rather be three feet below the hole than eighteen inches above it. Uphill I will go more boldly from fifteen feet because the putt stops more quickly.

In all putting you are confronted by two truths difficult to reconcile. If you don't get the ball up it can't go in. But for each added bit of speed it has less of the hole to hit. On some days I used to watch Denny Shute batting putts five feet past the hole (those that didn't go in, I mean), and after he had calmly knocked the five footers back in I would conclude that he really had *the method*. Undoubtedly this was one reason why he had such an excellent match-play record. A style like that is not easy on the opponent's nerves. But there were other days when Denny three-putted himself right out of tournaments, and in medal play there is no mental rabbit punch quite like a three-putted green.

Bobby Jones, on the other hand, tried to get even the shortest putts to die right at the hole, where if they touched any part of the rim they dropped. Probably the most famous putt in American golf was one like this, made by the master himself. It just barely got to the seventy-second hole and tumbled in on the high side to tie him with Al Espinosa for the 1929 National Open at Winged Foot. Coming as it did at the end of a collapse on Jones' part, during which he had apparently thrown away the tournament, that putt seemed to end his near-great days and point toward his grand slam of the next year. The following day in the play-off he took a double bogey on the first hole, spotting Espinosa two strokes right there, but then proceeded to beat him by twenty-three shots. If the putt on the seventy-second hole had stopped one roll short, he himself admits that he might have chucked the whole pursuit of major championships forever.

So decide for yourself how you are going to putt, and then stick to your system. Move my arbitrary fifteen feet in or out as you please, but have a clear idea of when you want to lag and when you want to make sure the ball gets to the hole. However I see nothing but comic relief when a player knocks a twenty-foot putt ten feet by the hole and then says, "Well, at least I gave it a chance."

The bold putters, of course, capture the imagination. At a recent Masters I was paired with one: the Japanese star, Nakamura. He was reputed to be so deadly and bold that Jimmy Demaret and others were betting on him to out-putt me in that round. Horton Smith was taking all the wagers they offered. Well, it was no contest, not because Nakumura wasn't good or might not have beaten me on other greens, but because on the slick, sloping, huge greens at Augusta his boldness was sheer suicide. The lag putt there, from almost any distance, becomes a necessity.

Practicing your putting is a tricky business. Though you should practice often, I don't think more than *fifteen* or *twenty minutes* at a time does you any good. The important thing is to practice enough to retain your confidence. Psychologically, putting has such a continuous, unrelenting effect on a player that a positive mental outlook is absolutely indispensable. You must tell yourself that on any single putt there are more variables than a genius can figure out and allow for, but that you will still hit it as you see it. For if you hit the putt with the speed you plan and on the line you envision, you have done your job perfectly no matter what happens to the ball.

In my estimation it was this sort of philosophy which made Horton Smith's great natural talent go so far. Say he was faced with a short sidehill putt which he decided would break two inches, if it just passed the hole. Well, if after hitting that putt correctly for such allowance he saw it miss on the high side, he would play the same relative break coming back. He had seen it that way, he would putt it that way. His stubborn, I'm-from-Missouri attitude resulted in a few three-putt greens here and there. But it was also part and parcel of the greatest putter I have ever seen, then or now. His mediocre days were good days for anyone else. And nobody matched his good days. The point is, he always putted them the way he saw them. Contrast Horton's confidence with that of the average player, who if he leaves a ten-foot uphill putt short on the first hole, will tell himself, "Boy, these greens are unusually slow," and then will spend the rest of the day going five or six feet past.

Confidence such as Smith displayed really pays a kind of compound interest. Suppose sometime you are confronted with very bumpy or very grainy greens. If you don't fully trust your stroke or your ability, you begin to worry about how these bad conditions will affect you. The man who knows what he's doing, on the other hand, and who trusts his putting, tells himself he'll be able to handle the rougher conditions better than anybody else. He even welcomes poor greens as being to his advantage relatively speaking. This may sound like poppycock, but I assure you it isn't. Once your putting fundamentals are sound, you can lean on them like that.

The nerves, of course, are always a major problem in putting; they are much harder to control here than in any other part of the game. But again, the sounder your style the more chance you give your nerves. The man who opens and closes the blade on every putt, and who keeps placing the ball in different positions is bound to get jumpier from his unpredictable results. Here, too, Horton Smith had a dictum that helped. Every putt, he said, was a straight putt. In his mind the player should simply *move the hole*. If Horton had to "borrow" two inches for a putt, he convinced himself that the hole was two inches from where it actually was, and tried to hit the ball straight for that imaginary target. But suppose instead of doing this you think about how the putt will break. You are quite likely to pull or push the ball as you strike it. Establishing this movable cup for putts that need some "borrowing" (moving it toward you going downhill, away from you going uphill) helps keep your stroke uniform.

Having said this, I must admit that some good putters, like Lloyd Mangrum, advise just the opposite. They actually change the position of the ball at address for a putt breaking one way or the other. Thus Mangrum hits a left-to-right breaking putt slightly in the heel of the putter to make it counteract the break. On a right-to-left putt, he hits it on the toe.

Jack White, too, an English putting authority, intentionally cut any putt which broke from right to left, to fight the slope, so to speak, and he hooked those that broke to his right (though in hooding the putter face for the hook he ran the risk of driving the ball down into the grass and, if it was long or grainy, bouncing back across the line). So I feel shadings of this sort, while useful in other shots, which we'll discuss later, complicate the putting process that should be standardized as far as is possible.

So to repeat what I said earlier, supinate the hands, and stay with that grip even for a month if it takes that long for it to become comfortable. Then you will be locking the clubface in place as much as a human being can while still making a rhythmic effort. Keep your stance square, place the ball uniformly just on the inside of the left shoe, and reduce your wrist action to the minimum by letting your forearms take charge of the stroke.

If in order to make sure that the putter face is at right angles to the line you must place it in front of the ball first, and then move it behind, do not be afraid to do so. Actually, though, you run some risk of changing the angle of the putter when you move it this way. You would be smarter to place the club behind the ball to begin with, if you can visualize it clearly enough there. But I for one have never been able to see the face well enough without first putting the clubhead in front of the ball. At any rate, don't make the change from front to back unless experience proves you have to. A simple tee-square on a rug will often show you whether you make mistakes in putter-face position.

Now if you feel these commands are too severe, that such terms as 'exactly square to the line," or "with the putter shaft parallel to the inside of the left shoe" ask you to be too much of an automaton, I'd rather concede you a margin of error on one side than on the other. I'd rather see a stance too closed, for example, than too open, or a putter coming inside out than outside in. I'd also rather see a ball played too far forward than too far back.

But in spite of much expert advice to the contrary, I do not like to see your hands in front of the ball when you address a putt. The major reason why Sam Snead has trouble with short putts seems to be this tendency to use a forward press with his hands just before taking the putter back. He does not do this on long putts and there he is very accurate.

Getting the hands ahead, or the ball either in the center of the stance or back toward the right foot, obliges you to hit the putt on the downswing, driving the ball down into the putting surface instead of across it. The putt then is more adversely affected by grain and bumpiness and is really going toward the hole on a bounce, because of being squeezed against the ground. On very smooth grain-free greens this tendency to bounce the ball may not be noticeable.

Reading greens correctly, of course, is essential, even if you are hitting your putts right. And here grain is a great complicator, especially in the Bermuda grasses. You can foretell some of the effect grain will have by observing its color. When the grain is against you, the grass looks darker; when it is with you the grass looks lighter. This affects not only the line and speed of the putt, but also the way you ought to strike it. On greens with very heavy grain you should make sure to get the ball up on top of the grass, by hitting the putt slightly on the upswing. In the extreme case of standing water on the greens you want to get the ball up even more quickly by actually using a two or three iron to putt with.

Many people these days are using the plumb-line device to line up their putts. I do not use it myself because I've never really had much trouble reading greens. But for those who do have difficulty seeing the breaks, it may help. Stand directly behind the ball, lining it up with the hole. Suspend the putter in front of you so that it hangs free, straight down. Sighting with one eye, cover the ball with the lower part of the putter shaft. Then, without moving the putter, or your head, look up at the hole. If it shows to the right of the shaft, for instance, your putt breaks right, by that amount. Or if the top of the shaft covers the hole, the putt is straight. I have asked professional surveyors about this method, and they say it is sound in principle. On seaside and mountain courses, where optical illusions play many tricks, it may come in especially handy.

This built-in equalizer of golf—putting, and the chipping and pitching which we'll discuss next—has been my bread and butter over many years. I still remember all the crucial putts I have made, or missed, and there have been plenty of both. The best one I made was also one of the very shortest: about a four footer in 1930 on the sand green eighteenth hole at Pinehurst, North Carolina. Knocking it straight in gave me my first major championship, the North South Open, which at that time was like the Masters now, our third most important tournament. I had another very long short putt at Buffalo in 1934—an eight footer on the thirty-eighth hole against Craig Wood for my first P.G.A. Championship. In each case, I tried to give my jumpy nerves just one message: trust your stroke. That really is always the best prescription. And, in spite of feeling that I might be ill on the spot, the trick worked.

However, the most amazing putting performance I ever put on

was not in a tournament at all. After the 1938 P.G.A. some newsreel cameramen came to Metropolis C.C., at White Plains, and asked me to exhibit my stock in trade. Would I kindly hole a few long putts for them, over hills and dales? I told them that if they didn't mind running out of film waiting for me to make one, I'd try. On the sixteenth green, I placed myself a good sixty-five or seventy feet from the cup, with full rolling contours between me and it, and told the boys to start grinding.

I expected to be there for quite a while. To my surprise I knocked in the very first putt dead center. It looked like a fixed performance, even to me. I made the next two also. The director wasn't a bit impressed.

I guess he thought that's what I was: a golf pro who dropped putts. So he merely asked me, "please, get the next one close, but don't knock it in." For they wanted a picture of the ball just barely missing the cup. Lo and behold, I stood my fourth effort on the very rim of the hole and that was that. Those cameramen went back to New York taking the whole thing for granted!

CHAPTER 7

CHIPPING

THE two ends of a golf game are the most important. Putting comes first, and driving, second. But a very close third in importance is the ability to get the ball down in two from immediately off the green, within chip-shot or short pitch-shot distance. Among our present-day stars no one does this better than Jerry Barber or Doug Ford. And in my hey-day I ranked myself in this respect second only to Johnny Revolta. Johnny probably had to be a little better, since he hit even fewer greens than I did. There is usually this criticism mixed in with any praise for skill in scrambling; we imply that the player could never get along on the rest of his golfing equipment. Yet, if the criticism bothers you, you can always scramble poorly, too, and lose.

Furthermore, there is one outstanding example of an excellent striker of the ball who was also very good at getting down in two whenever he had to: Ben Hogan himself. Probably no other fact testifies so well to the thorough-going discipline he brought to his game. To practice long and steadily enough to acquire mastery over a phase of play which represented such a relatively minor percentage of his shots took application in every sense of the word. But those of us who hit fewer greens must rely on these short shots to salvage par fours and to get birdies on par fives.

CHIPPING   45

To differentiate between chip and pitch shots: the chip shot requires variable loft and no reverse spin; the pitch shot requires variable loft *and* variable degrees of spin. And chipping, at least to me, covers those shots immediately off the putting surface, ranging from a few inches outside to perhaps twenty or thirty feet. Some loft is required, in order to carry the ball on the fly to the green itself, but backspin is not needed. The aim is just to hit the green safely and make the ball run from that point on toward the hole as much like a putt as possible. It seems logical then to use the putting grip and putting stroke. Except for unusual circumstances, such as when you must hit the ball through a narrow opening between two trees, the very outside limit for such a putting stroke is seventy or eighty feet. But as a youngster I discovered that from close in to the green it worked far better than either trying to chip with the conventional pitch shot grip or using the putter itself from the deeper grass.

There are important differences, of course. You have to keep your hands ahead of the ball on chip shots, unlike putts, since the ball is not sitting up and must be struck before the bottom of the arc is reached to insure a clean contact even in fuzzy fairway grass. A six iron is the straightest-faced club I ever use, although I do lead the clubhead with the hands sometimes far enough to reduce it, probably, to a four-iron loft. Why don't I simply use the four iron? Because then my hands would be even with the ball and I would be more likely to hit behind it. That is the major sin in these greenside shots. For then the shot will usually expire right in front of you. However a ball that is half-topped can still turn out fairly well because this method gives a wider margin for error.

In the days when we could carry as many clubs as we wished, the ideal chipper was the jigger, with its shallow blade and more curved sole than the regular irons. That curved sole helped keep the blade from digging. If the fourteen-club rule is ever repealed that jigger would be the first club to go back into my golf bag.

So instead of chipping with the conventional grip, or putting the ball from off the green through different textures of grass, the putter grip with lofted clubs, and the putter stance, with modifications, is the answer. (Fig. 12). The ball is played in the center of the stance, instead of opposite the inside of the left shoe. And the weight is about sixty-five percent on the left foot, instead of being evenly distributed. And you still do not have your hands the same degree in front of the ball for every shot. It is up to you to decide how much loft you need. From one club to the other the change in loft is three degrees. At thirty feet or so, this change in loft probably represents six feet difference in run, and we obviously must be more precise than that.

But if you have a clear picture of what you're trying to do, a little trial and error will soon make many of your decisions automatic. Judge what trajectory will carry the ball safely onto the putting surface to run the rest of the way toward the hole. Then decide how much loft on what club will produce that trajectory, and how far down the shaft you should grip the club to hit the shot that far.

Going uphill, with little distance between me and the edge of the green and plenty of running room on it, I will hold my hands farthest ahead, using the six iron.

Going downhill, however, my hands would be only far enough ahead to make sure I didn't hit the ground first. If the clubhead angle of the six iron with the hands slightly ahead would make the ball run too far, I would change to a more lofted club, even to the wedge, if necessary, so that I would be almost nudging the ball on the green to run down the slope of its own dead weight. *In no case would I risk scooping it.*

If I were afraid the ball would not stop soon enough, with even the most lofted club, I would resort either to a pitch shot with plenty of cut (which we'll discuss in the next chapter) or to a chip designed to hit in front of the green and run onto it.

I apply my chipping method to almost one hundred percent of the shots that are not actually on the putting surface itself. I don't even putt a ball that is only two or three inches off the green, unless it is sitting so high in the grass that it should reach the putting surface on the fly. It is, of course, common practice

CHIPPING 47

FIG. 12

these days—even among the experts—to use a putter from well off the green. But I still regard this as a confession of weakness in chipping. The weakness stems, in my opinion, from using the conventional grip and stroke on such shots, instead of the putting grip and stroke.

I am mildly amazed, as a matter of fact, at how many of the world's great players seem to neglect adapting the putting method to these shots. The additional fact that two of them do not neglect it, and that those two are Ben Hogan and Arnold Palmer, does not seem without significance either.

The putting grip, as I have said, should be used. But I overlap differently for the chips, going back to the standard Vardon overlap, instead of the reverse overlap that I use in putting. Yet if pressed for some overpowering reason why I do this, I couldn't give it to you. After all, the stance is square, the stroke is in the arms, with the shoulders turning only so far as they have to for the force required. (Fig. 13). The wrists should be kept out of the shot entirely. So overlapping one way or the other, or even using the eight-fingered grip, should make no difference.

As to why we must have the feeling of hitting these chips and putts with the forearms, I would cite the examples of Leo Diegel and Bill Mehlhorn. Both were fine hitters of the ball. Playing with "Wild Bill" once (a nickname that fitted only his short game), I watched him hit every green in regulation figures and every par-five in two. From tee to green he was four under par. Yet he made a seventy-three, and I with *twelve* putts less, made a sixty-nine. Bill was a hardy soul, somehow able to stand the ruin these sudden wristy-putting and chipping lapses spread through otherwise superlative rounds. But at any time his wrists might snap uncontrollably and would send the ball almost anywhere. These twitches happened sometimes right next to the hole. I once saw him carry an eight-foot putt past the cup on the fly, to run fifteen feet or so off the green.

Leo Diegel, with much the same problem, came nearer to solving it. He finally worked out a winged-elbow style, keeping his forearms parallel with the ground. This effectively kept his wrists

CHIPPING 49

FIG. 13

from flipping on him. Sarazen says that you could always tell where Leo had recently played exhibitions. Members could be seen bending over and around every green with their hands up against their chests.

Of course, you can't eliminate all break of the wrists. Probably the weight of the clubhead swinging will cause them to break a little. This break, however, should not be consciously or deliberately produced.

When we come to the problem of telling you how hard to hit any particular chip we again approach the unteachable. Yet there are still ways to help yourself, and general rules to observe. The longer the chip the firmer the grip. You also shade the force of the stroke by how far down the shaft you grip the club. But the length of the stroke itself is not proportional to the ball's distance from the hole. If a six-inch stroke knocks the ball six feet, it will take less than a twelve-inch stroke to knock it twelve feet. But the grip gets tighter and the tap firmer.

Practice alone produces the actual feel of distance. And it's always tentative, with the eyes themselves playing a major role. It has never helped me, for instance, to walk up to the hole and back on a long putt or long chip. Looking at the shot from the other side of the hole really confuses me more than it helps. Still I have seen players with problems of sight, who did get an idea—in one player's case his only real idea—of the distance to the hole by walking up to it and back again. This may be a time-consuming habit for some, but for that man it was a necessity. And he became a passable chipper and putter without ever really seeing how far away he was.

Instead of taking long surveys I use a bowling technique. A bowler selects a spot in the alley that he wants the ball to hit first, knowing that if he sets himself at the right angle and starts the ball there it will go where he wants it. Similarly, in chipping, I pick out a spot on the green for the ball to hit safely with the particular trajectory I desire. If I succeed in hitting reasonably near that spot I know the run will be about right. Greens, of course, are not bowling alleys. They can slope toward you, away from you, or to one side or the other. So the spot to aim at is movable, not always in line with the hole, and it is always a matter of judgment.

Here, too, I try not to be too demanding. From eighty feet away a four-and-a-quarter inch cup can seem like a pretty hopeless target. So from that distance I surround it with an imaginary five-foot ring for the ball to stop in. Such a wider circle seems to give me more leeway, and if I really roll the ball to a stop in the ring, the longest putt I can have will be two and a half feet. As I get nearer the hole I keep shortening the ring a bit. But on any and all chips I expect to get down in two, with the few short chips I hole making up for those I don't get close enough to one-putt.

And yet in spite of this boast, the chip I still remember most vividly is one that didn't come off. In the Miami Biltmore Open of 1932 I came to the par-five seventy-second hole needing a birdie to tie Sarazen for the lead. A three-foot uphill putt on the hole before had hit the very back of the cup at moderate speed and jumped up on the high back edge to stand there, after I had stubbed a fifteen footer to leave me short three feet. Binding me a little tighter was the fact that there was nobody in the world whom I would rather have beaten at that point than Sarazen. He had tossed off so many outspoken verdicts (Runyan was too frail ever to win a major event, for example) that I was anxious, or perhaps over-anxious, to make him eat a few of them.

Trying as hard as I could to get a tie, I hit two good woods around the dogleg four-hundred-and-ninety-yard eighteenth. This left me just off the green and no more than twenty feet from the pin. And I'd bet anybody even money that I could get down in two (nine times out of ten) from there.

Taking out my light-headed jigger, I hit the shot as well as I knew how. But I hadn't seen an old ball mark on the green. My low flying chip, which had to run close to the hole, hit this unrepaired mark and jumped straight up in the air. I was left with a fifteen footer, instead of a fifteen incher. I ticked the hole with my putt, but the ball stayed out. The Squire of Brookfield Center had won again.

In time I came to realize that his bristling manner and remarks hid some inner insecurity of his own, as well as fine qualities which he didn't want to show. And in the long run the psychological pressure he put me under helped me more than it hurt me, especially later, when I came up against rugged men like Craig Wood and Sam Snead who made my physical inferiority much more obvious.

I use this incident principally to illustrate the danger of old ball marks. Fix them.

CHAPTER 8

THE PITCH SHOTS

IF the chipping range runs to about twenty-five feet off the green, the pitch shot takes over from there out to a hundred yards or so. Either backspin or height, or both, then become necessary to hold the ball on the putting surface after it hits. The reason may be that the pin is very near the edge of the green, but usually it is that we are farther away. For if we are near the edge of the green and the pin is likewise, we can always resort to the chip shot which hits short and runs on. From farther away, letting the ball hit short is not advisable at all, unless absolutely necessary. Too many unpredictable things can happen on the bounce.

For the pitch shots we return to the regular, orthodox grip, where the "V" of the left hand points to the right shoulder and the "V" of the right hand points at the nose. The club is held by a semi-palm, semi-finger grip of the left hand, and by a finger grip of the right. But the grip of the right hand is more relaxed than that of the left. In putting and chipping, you remember, it has been equally firm.

Most of the shots calling for backspin are played with the nine iron or pitching wedge, or the sand wedge itself if only one wedge is carried. For the loft on these clubs is enough to allow us to pinch the shot slightly and still get enough height to hold the ball on the green. The stance is more erect than for the chip shots,

54 THE PITCH SHOTS

FIG. 14

since the left arm is now straightened out. (Fig. 14). The ball is played opposite the center of the body, or just in front of center. The weight stays fifty-five or sixty percent on the left foot, so that the hands are slightly ahead of the clubhead when it is placed behind the ball.

My body is turned fractionally toward the hole, in what could be called an open stance except for the fact that the heels are still square to the line. I turn the left toe toward the hole to help keep my weight forward, but this sets up a slightly outside-to-in swing path (Fig. 15). Thus, if my hand action is correct, there will be a trace of fade to the shot, or at least it will eliminate a tendency to hook.

Only in extreme cases (with the ball sitting up on a tuft of grass, for instance) would the stance be closed, to keep the shot down, or to hook and run it back into the left hand corner of a green if there is plenty of room in front.

As you swing back the weight is retained wholly on the left foot. The shoulder pivot which takes place and the accommoda-

THE PITCH SHOTS

FIG. 15

ting turn of the hips merely transfers the weight from left heel to left toe, and back to the heel again on the downward stroke. There should be no lateral shift to the right foot. For on these shots you want to make sure the club catches the ball on a downward arc. The pinching action causes the ball to run up the club face and be gripped by the grooves there to produce backspin. From a horizontal hit the ball would fly off the club face sooner and you would get no backspin.

In pitching, the backswing should be a bit firmer than in the fuller shots, in direct ratio to the length of swing. If you make a swing that is twenty-five percent full, you manage only a twenty-five percent cock of your wrists. For a half-swing, the wrists cock half-way; in a three-quarter swing, three-fourths of the way. You must maintain this ratio of arm to wrist swing.

Otherwise, if your arms travel through only a quarter of their normal arc, for example, and your wrists still break fully, you will probably go past the ball on your downswing before your hands ever catch up. And even if they did catch up the result would be too powerful.

So, the arms return to the ball with the wrists from this more limited cock. You then have a natural follow-through. Its length depends not only on the fullness of the backswing, but also upon how much turf has been taken in hitting the shot.

Your head must stay meticulously still, both vertically and laterally. For the remark, "I looked up," really does not always apply. A badly topped or skulled shot can be caused by your head simply moving *forward*, whether it moves *up* or not.

And the phrases, "I looked up," or "I peeked," uttered by someone who has just taken a slab of earth a foot behind the ball would be true in only one special way. What caused you to hit the ground before you got to the ball was a ducking of your head and shoulders before contact, usually on the backswing. You may, of course, have ducked so far down that even if you did look up you would still be too low, and would still hit behind the ball. In that case, "I looked up," would be a true statement, but actually not the cause of the digging. The fault was the droop, not the jump upward to recover.

I have actually seen players dip in this way going back, then look up on their way down and—with the errors providentially cancelling each other out—somehow hit the shot quite squarely. At such times I never heard one of them say, "I looked up," though the statement would have been perfectly true.

So the error of moving the head and shoulders can be made in *any direction* and any such movement seriously multiplies your timing problems. I must admit it is possible, however, to become so tense in trying to hold your head rigidly still over the ball that your swing becomes too restricted. But a sound program for fixing and maintaining this central focus, which I saw Arnold Palmer use recently, is to pay particular attention to holding your head still in all practice sessions, even at the risk of missing shots. After leaving the practice tee, in the actual round that followed, Arnold did not continue this exaggerated manner of holding his head down over the ball. But his practice session still had a good carry-over effect.

As I have said, your body does turn as you go back on these shots, and so the clubface does not remain in a fixed position with relation to the ball, as in a putt or a chip. Yet the clubface does stay in a fixed position with relation to the body. If on a pitch your shoulders, say, turn ten degrees to hit the shot, the face of the club has also opened ten degrees with relation to the ball. In relation to the shoulders or body, however, it is still square. In other words, there has been no pronation or supination of the wrists, independent of the body turn.

All the way up to the power shots the process is the same. If the shoulder turn or pivot is a full ninety degrees, or even more, the clubface opens by that full amount, and that amount only. Its position with relation to the shoulders is still the same as it was at address. I want to hammer at this point to eliminate any confusion about my advocating an open-to-closed swing. The word "pronation" in this respect seems to cause misunderstanding. Let me repeat that the wrists never open the clubface by themselves. Body turn does it (or more particularly shoulder turn, since on fuller shots they turn farther than the hips). Yes, it is *body turn alone* which opens the face, and then only with relation to the ball.

On the downswing the body, arms and wrists return to their original position, not stopping there, of course, but going on through. On these pitch shots you must avoid all feeling of trying to help the ball up into the air. The loft on the face of the club automatically takes care of this for you.

The grip should be kept crisp enough to make for precision (although later we'll discuss a type of shot where a certain amount of looseness, or even sloppiness, is required). Shots of average height and average spin call for firmness, with the wrists uncocking only to their original position, and not past it in any sort of scoop. As the arms swing on by the only subsequent wrist motion would be caused by the club's momentum, and not by any conscious effort of the hands.

In any of these shots, your swing must match what the blade of your club is doing. This may sound too trite to mention. But once you run down the list of alternate trajectories and degrees of spin it is well to keep it in mind. For example, if I have the blade of my club exactly at right angles to the desired line of flight, my swing should also be going directly at the hole, assuming that there is no wind or slope to make other allowances necessary. But if I hold the blade one degree open, in order to give spin or cut to the shot, I must swing directionally one degree to the left of the target to match this cut. Aiming four or five degrees to the left, I must obviously cut the shot more; by allowing my hands to make the heel of the clubhead go through the ball ahead of the toe.

So you handle the intentional allowance for cut by the position of your feet, and you handle the degree of cut in executing the shot by the way you use your hands in hitting the ball and also by the angle at which you set the clubface in the address position. The point—which we made before in our chapter on the stance—is to be sure that if you have set yourself up to allow for a cut, your hands execute it properly in the hitting area. If from an open stance you allow the blade to come back at right angles to that stance, or the toe to pass the heel, you will end up with the equivalent of a snap hook for this length of shot, and the ball will go over to the left and probably much too far as well.

I am not urging you to change the swing plane for each of these swings. You adjust it directionally by your stance, depending upon how you plan your hand action in coming through the ball. By and large, the swing should remain on its natural arc, fractionally more upright for pitch shots simply because the weight is held more on the left foot than the right.

Of equal importance to this sort of directional control is the choice and management of trajectory. Just as there are degrees of cut, or absence of cut entirely, depending upon how much spin or stopping action is desired, so there are degrees of pinch with which any pitch shot can be hit, depending upon how low we want the ball to fly.

Before we go into them, however, I want to make sure you don't confuse the terms "pinch" and "punch." "Pinch" refers exclusively to the arc of a swing. How much "pinch" is put on a shot depends entirely on how much it is hit on the downswing. "Punch," on the other hand, describes the kind of swing itself. Punchers use little or no wrist action, whether they are striking the ball on the downswing, at the bottom of the swing, or even on the upswing. But punchers still do not pinch every shot, by any means, though their lack of wrist action makes even their lobs fly a little lower than the more loosely flipped lobs of wristier swingers. For in some situations a lobbing action may be desired instead of a pinch. Then instead of striking the ball a descending blow the clubhead makes contact at the very bottom of its arc and produces a higher flight.

But we are discussing a whole series of choices here which only particular circumstances can make clear. Generally speaking, with pins anywhere from the middle to the back of greens, pinch shots are used, because the ball has room to stop from a lower trajectory. But once in a while a pinch shot will be used when the pin is on the very front, if the wind is so strongly in your face, for example, that even a low shot will be cushioned to stop abruptly. A high lob under those conditions might be coming down backwards by the time it reached the green, and thus not get there at all.

Still, with the pin near the front edge of the green, and the air calm, you want a higher-flying, more steeply dropping shot, like a mortar shell. And to hit such a lob you must adjust your weight differently. Instead of holding it preponderantly on the left foot, it is kept evenly balanced. The ball is moved forward as well, so that the shaft of the club and the hands, instead of being ahead of the ball are exactly even with it. The arc of your swing, because of this different weight distribution, will be slightly less upright. The club hits the ball at the bottom of the arc and causes it to rise more quickly.

This is a shot which requires a reasonably good lie. From either a cuppy or a bare lie there would be too much danger in this sort of lob stroke catching the ground behind the ball, digging into the grass if the ground were soft, or bouncing the club into the back of the ball and skulling it if the ground were hard. From such lies the ball must be hit a descending blow regardless of the lower trajectory it causes. And some height and stopping action could still be obtained by cutting it.

So the pinch is your low, fairly hard-flying shot with lots of spin to stop it. The lob is your high-flying, steeply-dropping shot used when the pin is close to the front of a green, or just behind a bunker. In such cases you do not want to risk landing short, but if the ball strikes near the hole with a lower trajectory it will run too far, in spite of having fractionally more spin. The new wedges help bring off the high lob more easily, with their rounded soles which enable the clubhead to cup under the ball. We will discuss that subject more fully in the chapter regarding proper equipment.

Having gone over the lob and the pinch, we now come to the question of what degree of cut should be applied to them in what circumstances. The pinch-cut is used when loft is needed, but when the lie is not good enough to try the lob. You want a high trajectory, but your lie won't allow it. So your weight is held well forward, to strike the ball a descending blow. The face is opened to make the shot come up fairly quickly. This calls for a stance adjustment. Again, in the actual stroke you have to be sure that your hands keep the heel of the clubface ahead of the toe, so that the cut is executed.

The lob-cut, on the other hand, combines both height and stopping action. It is the shot which, barring wind conditions, travels the least from the point it strikes. Unfortunately, it is also the hardest to control. The ball is slipping sideways on the clubface at impact in addition to flying off more quickly. It is a wise player, indeed, who knows the maximum amount of cut he can apply to such a lob without having the ball slip off the face altogether and go nowhere.

You do not have an open stance with the straight lob, but you do with the lob-cut. Your weight does not shift forward, but stays evenly balanced, with your head opposite the ball. Your wrists are a little more supple in the stroke, breaking a little more forward than they do for the pinch. The stroke also has to be a little longer than for a pinch hit the same distance. The fact that the shot goes higher dissipates some of its power. I cannot lob a ball with a nine iron more than a hundred yards, unless the wind is behind me. But I can pinch it up to a hundred-and-ten- or fifteen- yards.

So the cut shot can be either a lob-cut or a pinch-cut. Obviously, there are infinite shadings to each. And practice alone will enable a player to develop finesse in dealing with them. But he does have to understand the fundamentals first. After a while the expert becomes so proficient that he acquires something like the touch of a pianist hitting the right note and with the right emphasis. With a given club he can change the amount of pinch for a particular shot simply by shifting his weight slightly one way or the other. He has learned just how far forward he can lean without topping the ball, and how far back he can position his head for the lob without hitting the ground first.

But even a player accomplished in these techniques often finds them difficult to reproduce with any set of clubs but his own. And when he breaks in new clubs he has to learn anew all the variable effects of these slightly different tools, even when they are manufactured to specifications he has asked for and checked.

Learn to make these pitch shots do your bidding, and keep practicing what you have learned, to maintain your feel. For even though I have had to understand them thoroughly to play in the big leagues at all—I am not well-enough practiced in them right now to bring them off as I wish, when I wish. Just the same, given a week or two to polish up my pitches, I could get them down to a very fine tolerance, because I know their causes and effects. So long as a mathematician grasps the principles upon which he's operating, he can make his problem work by going back and checking over it even if he's made a mistake somewhere along the line. So here, too, if we have the fundamentals straight, we can tell ourselves what went wrong with any specific shot and correct it next time. Additionally, we can put together a more thorough technique which helps us become more versatile.

It's not only a matter of hitting the ball right either. Once you can produce a full range of these pitch shots, you still have to judge when certain ones are best used. As in chipping, you must suit club selection to the particular carry and roll desired, and to your lie. Furthermore, all greens obviously do not act alike. They are not the same size, shape, or depth, and do not have the same texture, even when uniformly watered. The experienced player must learn to read these variations.

If the green has been heavily watered, for instance, but the surface has been kept short and clipped, it would probably be best to play a fairly high shot with a modest amount of backspin —a very light pinch, or a lob—especially if the green slopes at all towards you.

But if the greens are hard, and if to preserve them the greens-keeper has let the grass grow fairly long to build up the nap, you will have a better chance of stopping the ball with maximum spin, rather than height.

A green that is both very hard and very slick may defy any

shot that hits there on the fly to stay on it. You then have to resort to the pitch-and-run. Specifically, this is a lob, which pitches short of the green and runs onto it, but it is executed with a straighter-faced club than is normally used for pitching. Out of necessity the shot becomes much more imprecise, but the principles are the same.

In summary, as you keep your weight forward the ball goes lower, whether you are using a wedge or a straighter-faced club. As you equalize weight distribution, the ball goes higher: highest with the wedge, with the least roll; less high with the eight and nine irons, with more roll. So if with the wedge I have my weight evenly balanced and the ball still does not go high enough, I do not lean farther back on my right foot. That would make me bounce the club behind the ball. I would begin to lob-cut it instead.

And finally, just as it is helpful in chipping to pick out a spot on the green for the ball to hit, so on these pitches particular spots can be useful guides to proper trajectory. Only now, the spots are located up and down the flagstaff instead of laterally along the green. As a general rule, if I'm hitting a pinch shot of average height and average severity, I aim for the middle of the flag. If I'm trying to play an unusually low shot I aim for the bottom, right at the cup. In trying to play a lob, I aim for the top of the flag.

Of course, in setting these flight patterns wind conditions are a major influence. If the wind were against me and I still decided I had to hit a lob, I would aim over the flag, to make sure and get the ball there. For a lob with the wind behind me, I would aim at the foot again. And for a pinch-cut with the wind against me I might aim for somewhere near the top.

Anyone who has been lucky enough to see Johnny Revolta dancing the ball up there around the hole with these shots will appreciate his artistry. With a little old fast swing that sometimes barely got the full shots off the ground, Johnny turned more seventy-nines into sixty-nines with great pitch shots from under a hundred and twenty-five yards than any man I ever saw.

But famous professionals aren't the only ones who know how to pitch. Nor should they be, since here the great divider—power—draws no distinction. True, one player is able to put much more backspin on his short pitch shots than another. But he does so not because he is stronger, or "gets more wrist action," as is often said—at least, not in the sense of turning his wrists into the ball. He obtains greater spin by hitting the ball more precisely, with a more vertical stroke which holds the ball against the face of the club longer. He catches the ball just below center and causes it to run up all the grooves. It is his dexterity in striking the shot this way which produces the greater spin and control—not wrist snap or strength itself.

I still remember Bill Taverner, a club member at Annandale C.C. in Pasadena, where I used to be resident professional. He became a four handicapper without often hitting more than six or seven greens a round. I have actually seen him make even par, hitting only three greens, without making sea-going putts either. No matter where his second shots went—and at Annandale, I assure you, this could be pretty wild, hopeless-looking country—shooting out of brambles or rough, or back to small, high greens sloping away from him, Bill would always hit the lob or sometimes the lob cut. And the ball rarely wound up more than four or five feet away. He never pinched the ball on these pitches; this sometimes made him less effective in high wind. But he was certainly a wedge master, if there ever was one, and that one shot almost miraculously redeemed the rest of his game.

Incidentally, I have praised Hogan for forcing himself to learn this department of play thoroughly, in spite of his few calls upon it. But the lob was one shot he did seem a little hesitant about. And though it was primarily his putting which balked his magnificent try for an unprecedented fifth Open at Cherry Hills in 1960, the shot that literally crumpled him was one such lob across the water on the seventeenth hole, which hit no more than a few inches short and cost him the tournament right there.

There is also the famous case of Sam Snead at Hillcrest in the Los Angeles Open. Needing to lob the ball up the hill from just below the eighteenth green to win, he left it short four times. Four times the ball rolled back down again to stop at his feet.

So these are always delicate shots, dependent upon feel, and susceptible to pressure and nerves. To minimize jumpiness about them, learn their dynamics thoroughly to bring them off. They offer golden opportunities to save strokes, or literally whole rounds. But if they remain total mysteries and if each effort brings some surprise, look out. For the only shot which, misunderstood, creates more havoc is the sand shot. Coincidentally, we will discuss that now.

CHAPTER 9

BUNKER SHOTS

TO get out of a bunker (which is the historical name for sand trap), and to get out of it well, should really be very simple. Properly understood, the explosion is the easiest of shots to make. Yet if you don't know the proper technique, it can be fiendishly difficult. And there is no middleground.

I would prefer to have my ball forty feet away from the hole in an ordinary bunker lie than behind that bunker on a perfectly good grass lie ninety feet away. I would rather have a short explosion shot of twenty-five feet from a bunker than a putt of sixty feet. For the modern-day sand club should take most of the guess work out of playing these shots, provided you have a technique that is reasonably good.

The wedges now have a high front lip which gives them a sled-runner effect, to slide through the sand just beneath the surface rather than to dig into it too deeply. The flange does not necessarily have to be broad. A highly inverted, but narrow, sole line is actually better. The front edge of the club, in other words, is up at an eight or ten degree angle from the trailing edge, but at the same time this sole is narrow enough so as not to make the front edge stick up too high off the ground. This high inversion on a narrow flange, rather than a low inversion on a broad flange, also enables you to use the club for pitches up to sixty or sixty-five

BUNKER SHOTS 67

FIG. 16

FIG. 17

yards. For those of us who carry five woods, seven irons and a putter, this sort of double duty from the wedge becomes necessary. But I also believe this particular design works better for sand shots.

The grip is standard, the same as for all the other shots but chipping and putting. The only basic difference in the swing for bunker shots concerns the arc. In the normal swing we have a well-rounded arc, but in the sand we want a "U" or even a "V" shaped one. Your arms actually bend a little. You don't make any attempt to extend them in a normally wide arc. And the shorter the shot the narrower the "V" should become. If you're playing a bunker shot where you want to jump the ball out of the trap only four or five feet, you narrow the "V" so much that you're practically swinging straight up and straight down. I'd like to call this special arc entirely "V" shaped. But it is true that for the longer bunker shots of sixty, seventy and eighty feet a slightly more-rounded one is required.

However, the swing for *all bunker* shots should be sharply vertical. This is my major point and for some reason the hardest to get across to pupils. So let's be sure you understand what is meant by a sharply vertical swing.

At address the ball is positioned opposite the left arch (Fig. 16), since we want to hit sand first and then contact the ball past the normal bottom of the swing. The center of gravity is a little behind the ball itself, though slightly forward of the particular spot in the sand we intend to strike, usually an inch and a half or two inches behind the ball.

To insure heavy contact with the sand the club is picked up abruptly back of the ball by a combined arm and wrist motion which describes one side of the "V" we have talked about (Fig. 17). Having been taken up on this arc, of course, the clubhead must then come down on the same steep path to pin-point accurately the spot we want to hit. If you go up gradually and come down abruptly you'll hit too far behind it. Or if you go up quickly and down gradually you will top the shot. So you must groove this side of the "V" by practice. You do have, however, a relatively

BUNKER SHOTS 69

FIG. 18

wide margin for error, wider at least than for any other shot in the game.

The face of the club should be kept a degree or two open at address, to guard against the front lip of the wedge ever getting lower than the trailing edge. If that happened the clubhead would continue to go downward as it hit the sand. For the front edge acts like the point of a plow. When the plow handles are raised, the point goes down into the ground.

Instead we want the special sole of the wedge to bruise its way under the ball, like the farmer pushing down on the handles to raise the point above the bed, causing the team to pull it out of the ground. If you have preserved the sled-runner or ploughshare feature, hitting down into the sand heavily, and almost vertically, still does not make the club go too deeply under the ball and leave it in the bunker. As a matter of fact it reverses the motion for you and starts the clubhead back upward.

Now during the stroke itself, as you go through the ball, the toe of the clubhead must never pass the heel. In coming up on the other side of the "V" you must be particularly careful never to let the wrists turn over. Since you give this shot considerable vigor, the left arm should begin to bend as you hit behind the ball in order to keep the clubface open as it skids under the cushion of sand. The elbow continues to break so that at the finish, the left forearm has not gone around to its usual semi-vertical follow-through position, but remains nearly horizontal. (Fig. 18). This action of the left arm, let me emphasize again, keeps the club from digging when it is thrown down from the first side of the "V."

If the player, instead of blocking any turnover of the toe past the heel, allows the wrists to snap as the clubhead starts under the ball, his only chance of not digging too deeply is to pull upward, or try to scoop the ball out. Nine times out of ten this results in a skulled shot which is even more disastrous. On the other hand, when you have held the clubface slightly open, and have maintained its sled-runner effect by letting the left elbow break upon the club's contact with the sand, it will practically bounce out.

You go along with it then in a pronounced follow-through much as you would go along with the spring of a diving board.

The explosion shot may be long enough to demand a pivot, and if it does, you must take special care to see that your head remains in a fixed position. (Your weight should be evenly balanced or slightly forward on the left foot.) For the only other real bunker trouble you can have in such a shot is to lose this focus, or hub, of the swing. Since the "V" is fairly narrow to begin with, you can't move the hub backward or forward, up or down, by letting your head sway or dip, without risking failure. The generous margin for error we've talked about does not include that sort of movement.

Of course, you find variable sand textures, just as you find different kinds of greens, and you have to learn the adjustments they call for. All types of sand are not equally porous. In firm, tightly packed sand, with less cushion between you and the ball, don't swing quite as hard as you would in the fluffier variety. (I prefer changing the force of the swing itself to moving the spot in the sand which you intend to hit.) Wetness, with any type of sand, has this effect: it packs the sand so that a blow of the usual force will make the ball fly farther.

I realize some bunker artists believe in moving the place in the sand where they want to hit. But I think you will simplify and standardize your procedure if you change only the force of your swing, easing it slightly for firm-packed or wet sand.

The only time you must vary the place you aim for is when the ball is buried, and then you should use either a pitching wedge or a nine iron. The distance you now hit behind the ball depends on how deep it is embedded. Like cutting a rotten spot out of an apple, the deeper the ball goes the farther around it you must cut. If it is only half-buried, you may be able to hit only an inch or so away from it and still get the ball out.

But for extracting any buried ball you should not use the sand wedge. You need greater penetration than it affords, unless you turn the toe in, as we have told you not to do for a normal lie.

Lloyd Mangrum advocates this hooding method for playing

buried balls in bunkers, and, of course, that is certainly one way to make the wedge dig. My main objection is that by turning the toe in you take off too much loft. This is all right except when you have to get the ball up and out to a green much higher than you are.

The nine iron, or pitching wedge, however, gets down to the ball without sacrificing elevation, for its lip is already lower than its trailing edge anyway. You play the shot in the same manner as you do with the wedge. But the ball will not act the same way after it hits the green. You can not get any spin on your shot from such an embedded lie. You must allow for more roll.

Bunker shots between seventy and a hundred-and-twenty feet long are the toughest. This is the mongrel distance: too far to explode, too short to cut out with a pinched nine iron. Unless the bank of the trap is too high, I prefer the cut nine iron beyond seventy feet. But if the ball has to rise sharply, the explosion must be tried.

Even in fairway traps when you are forty yards or farther from the hole, your problems are not serious, unless you must get the ball up quickly over a steep bank again. Barring that, you simply make sure the club first contacts the ball. If you keep your weight well-forward, the resulting half-topped or skulled shot is what you want. The only real miss occurs when the club hits the sand behind the ball. This rule holds true all the way to full bunker shots with the long irons, or even fairway woods.

When you get to these, however, the broader base of the clubhead itself can help you cut the ball out without so much chance of digging—if you make it spank the sand heel first.

In spite of the confidence you should have with sand shots, once you understand their principles, their dramatic dangers must be acknowledged, too. In a bunker by the green, you are so near, and yet so far. You either get out presentably or you don't. There's no in-between. Disasters, even among the experts, reach major proportions. (Like Palmer's blast on the eighteenth hole of the 1961 Masters, for example).

But the first National Open I ever played in featured perhaps the cruelest disaster, in the sense of being the most final. Along with ten thousand other people, I watched Roland Hancock blow an explosion shot too long from one bunker to the other on the seventy-first hole. He needed only a bogey and an easy par-five to win the tournament, the first Open he had ever played in. And he literally never recovered from that calamity, as a front-line competitor.

Sam Snead's eight on the last hole at Spring Mill in the 1939 Open, for all his many statements to the contrary, must have hurt him mentally in subsequent Opens. For he still needs to win this premier event to complete an otherwise stellar record. The memory of the lip of that fairway bunker catching his ball before it quite got up may well haunt him to this day.

I am not exempt, either. A bunker shot on the seventy-first hole of my 1933 Ryder Cup match against Percy Alliss still gives me as sharp a twinge of memory as any single shot I ever made. So much conspired to render it costly. I had been trailing Percy all day long and had finally caught him on the back nine of our afternoon round. We came to the next to the last hole even. Hitting before me, Percy put his shot on the fly into a bunker to the left of the green. Though the pin was to the right, I had to be cautious about hitting too boldly for it. Fifteen feet further to the right, down a slight bank, a small fence marked the out-of-bounds, near some railroad tracks. So I played too carefully away from this danger, and my ball rolled into the same bunker as Percy's. When we both got there we saw the two balls actually frozen together in the sand, near the back edge. His was found to be closer to the hole, and was marked, in accordance with the rules. Then I shot first. Since I had to stand on the grass of the bunker I could not test the sand's consistency with my feet (the exaggerated preparations of stance which players go through in bunkers can be just as much for sand inspection as for balance). I had no chance to discover that the sand was not uniformly porous, but had indeed a crust just underneath the surface. With the pin some sixty feet away, I thought I should take a fairly strong swing.

But the tight-packed sand made the ball fly past the flag. It rolled to the back of the green, trickled down the bank just under the fence and out-of-bounds. My shot told Percy all he needed to know. Although I got down in two with my next effort from the bunker, he was able to play safe for his five and win the hole.

But why, you may ask, fret so much over this one shot? Because Alliss and I tied the last hole that day, leaving me one down when my fifteen-foot birdie putt failed to go in. And because our American squad as a whole lost by one point. If I'd tied, we'd have tied; if I'd won, we'd have won. And also because in such team matches when you are representing your country, you feel you're letting down far more than just yourself.

On the plus side, I've also made many good, even thrilling, recoveries from bunkers to win tournaments. I remember one from a deep bunker at Echo Lake in the 1936 Metropolitan Open. As I neared the green to make my shot I saw Walter Hagen sitting up on the clubhouse veranda watching me. He had a smile on his face, and it seemed to say, "You're not going to get down in two, kid, and I'm going to beat you in the play-off." Well, I blew the shot out stone dead, and Sir Walter didn't get his play-off.

In that case, I read the texture of the sand correctly. But different types of sand are like different greens; you can't assume they are all going to be alike. In playing practice rounds on a strange course be sure and see whether there is any variation from one type of sand to the other and what that variation is.

There are general rules for these variations. Wetness, shallowness of sand, coarseness or crustiness, means that you must hit easier. And since tighter-packed sand will make the clubhead bounce more, you should also grip a little more tightly under such circumstances. Deep, soft, fluffy sand means, of course, that you must hit harder.

Remember then, this is an entirely different stroke than we use for any other shot. I have the devil's own time trying to get this vertical, up and down, concept across to most pupils. The usual error is too much flatness in the swing, then skimming the clubhead across the sand and picking the ball too clean.

If you don't want to explode the shot, assuming that there is no high front lip on the bunker and that you have plenty of running room on the green, the straight chip is workable enough. But make sure you stay forward over the ball to hit it first, and not the sand.

If, however, you have decided on the blaster, tell yourself you are driving that wedge down into the sand. In hammering a nail into a board, you would not swing horizontally. A vertical stroke, because of the specially inverted sole to the clubhead, will slide the blade under the ball. Even if you made no proper attempt to follow-through with your hands, the shot would probably still finish somewhere on the green, though that isn't what I recommend at all.

Finally, this sand-explosion technique can be used when you are not actually in a bunker. If you are on a bare lie immediately behind some hazard which you have to pitch over, you will be better off playing a regular sand shot, swinging easier and hitting a little closer to the ball, than you will be trying the pinch-cut, which is far more likely to be skulled too low.

From high greenside rough, also, something like this steep "V"-shaped stroke can be used, to avoid entangling the clubhead in six to eight inches of grass. Here, however, a ponderous, but slow-paced stroke, with an iron-like grip, as though you were swinging the club in slow motion, tears through the rough best. A lithe, fast stroke knocks the ball too far, and a lithe, slow one leaves it there. (Dutch Harrison has greater mastery of this shot than anybody I've ever seen, and I learned it from watching him.)

CHAPTER 10

THE MEDIUM IRONS

THE short control shots played with the nine iron or wedge are, of course, not full shots. They require variable kinds of english, from variable stances, producing variable trajectories.

In this chapter we will consider full shots with the clubs from the nine iron down to the five iron. This may not be the conventional division—of short, medium, and long irons—but it seems more natural to me.

We still need versatility with these shots, but the possible variations diminish as the club becomes more straightfaced. I have more alternatives of trajectory and spin, for example, with a nine iron than I have with an eight, and so on down the scale. This is noticeable especially on those shots requiring right to left flight. As loft decreases, the controlled hook is harder to hit.

Nevertheless, the basic fundamentals remain the same. On a full shot with the nine iron, where we are trying to get maximum power consistent with control, the standard Vardon grip is used.

The gripping strength, again, is mainly in the last three fingers of the left hand, with a diminishing degree of force from the heel of the left hand to the index finger and thumb of the right. The ball's position is just slightly to the left of center, with the weight sixty percent on the left foot. The stance is square in the case of a straight shot. And I take issue with golf books that state categorically the stance should be open *for a straight shot*. It may be that you want to fade eighty or ninety percent of the nine irons you hit, though this strikes me as a high percentage. If you do, you will certainly open your stance and make sure you cut the ball with your hands as you come through.

But in hitting the ball straight, or from right to left when the pin is far back in the left hand corner of a green, an open stance will multiply your problems. To get you inside the line going back, some sort of unnatural arm and shoulder action must take place, doing harm to the normal swing plane. The simpler solution is to change your stance.

So you come back a little inside the line, now, for the straight shot, with a fuller pivot which still does not transfer your weight completely to the right foot (Fig. 19). Your hands come up to a point somewhere above the right shoulder, opposite the curve of the neck. The swing itself, except for the variable planes we have already mentioned, determined by the different lengths of club, is a miniature of the fuller shots. The left side starts the backswing by turning toward the ball. Or if you want to say the right side turns away from the ball, I won't argue. One motion can't take place without the other. The left hand transmits the first hand motion to the clubhead, through the medium of the body turn. The grip end of the club thus moves fractionally before the clubhead itself, which finally leaves the ball. The sequence can be phrased any way you wish: left knee bending toward the ball, right knee straightening away from it; left shoulder turning toward it, right shoulder away. At any rate, the torque, or twist, of the body starts the backswing, and the hands deliver this motion to the clubhead. In the more bent-over position for a nine-iron shot, the pivot cannot be as full as for a drive without pulling your head off the ball or all your weight onto the right foot.

At the top of your backswing (though there really is no such absolute point), the left hip starts turning back toward the ball to initiate the downswing. It does so slightly before the clubhead itself has gotten all the way back, and exerts the pull or stretch on the muscles that contributes to the flexibility or slinginess of a

FIG. 19

good swing. The left arm controls this downward pull until the shaft is past horizontal on its way toward the ball.

This is where the hands themselves take over, with the final releasing or thrusting of the wrists which gets them out of the way of the speeding clubhead and squares it up to the ball again. Some players can delay this catching up of the hands and wrists longer than others, and can continue the left arm's pull well past the horizontal position of the club on its way down. Their hands are still so fast that they will not be late in getting the clubface squared up. But even the weakest player must wait until the shaft is below horizontal before initiating his hand action. If he does not, he will actually be casting the clubhead (and wasting its speed) away from the ball, not toward it.

As the player comes back to meet the ball, he again approximates the address position. The whip-like throw of his hands completes the squaring-up process, reaching the bottom of the arc slightly in front of the ball, where the head is held throughout the swing, unless a lob is being attempted. As the ball is met squarely, and as the body turns past the place where the hit has been made, the clubhead continues to swing also, through another cycle until with the shaft horizontally forward the face of the club has gone ninety degrees past its original position (a hundred and eighty degrees from the top of the swing). At this time all body turn has died out and the swing is completed on its proper plane, with the hands at about the same position over the left shoulder that they reached over the right shoulder during the backswing.

If such a swing, on such a plane, does not produce a straight shot (even though the grip was correct to start with), faulty hand action in the hitting area was responsible. The more you practice, the more automatic a reflex this becomes. And the more automatic or repetitious it becomes, the better off you are.

But we must admit that this is a game of intricate timing; and unfortunately bad habits can be learned and grooved too. If the right hand, for instance, grips too tightly, it cannot get out of the way of the clubhead, and ends up impeding clubhead action rather than triggering or releasing it. Deliberate concentration and thought, resulting in swings which for a while feel far from natural, may be necessary to break such a habit.

Muscular soreness, general fatigue, state of mind can all affect the way we swing. But generally—judging from my own experience—when you are beset by these timing problems you should sacrifice a little power for the sake of returning rhythm and smoothness to your swing. Often, when this is done, your hand action becomes synchronized again, and the swing gets back on the track, so to speak. The power then seems to return of its own accord, too.

You really can't devote too much time to hand action. After all, the clubhead does not naturally swing by the ball without being helped. A powerful pivot and stretch of the muscles at the top of the backswing creates enough speed for centrifugal force to take over on the way down. But once this speed has been created, the hands must turn through the ball, too, in order to stay out of the way of the clubhead.

Recent high-speed camera studies (which we'll discuss more thoroughly in the chapter on The Drive) have shown us that poorer players actually decelerate in the hitting area. So half the trick of getting good power lies in keeping the hands supple and flexible enough to help turn the clubhead through the ball once it has begun to move quickly. If I am playing an intentional fade, the arms are moving through their normal arc a little too fast for the hands to catch up. With the intentional hook, my arms move a little slower, so that the hands can not only catch up, but actually push the toe of the clubhead emphatically past the heel in the hitting area. In the straight shot, of course, the speed of arms and hands are meshed.

Now it may sound as though we're asking a great deal from our all-too-fallible faculties, and, of course, we are. But if you don't get proportionate satisfaction out of holding the game to a draw, say, in one or two cases out of a hundred, you're in the wrong sport. With a nine iron, for example, you've got to expect to do more than just get the ball on the green. You want to get close enough for a reasonable chance to one-putt. And to do so consistently you must appreciate the necessary shadings, not only in how to hit the shot, but also in what kinds of shots are most effective.

If, for instance, you're along the left edge of the fairway and the pin is near the left edge of the green, you still have additional surveys to make. What is to the left of the left edge—a steep bank or bunker? Does the green itself slope so sharply to the right that if the ball flew in straight it would run off to the right, anyway? In these cases, a little hook to the shot would be absolutely necessary to give you any chance at all of getting down in two.

Now everything we've already discussed about deliberate hooking comes into play. The feet are squared up to aim a bit to the right of the target. In relation to the target itself, this means a closed stance. But again, stance alone won't produce your hook for you. You have put yourself in a position where you can, and must, work your hands a little faster in the hitting area to make the ball drift slightly toward the pin from right to left in accordance with the allowance your stance has made for such hand action. Oddly enough, the clubhead itself is not accelerated by this action of the hands. Only the rotation of the toe past the heel is quickened.

Conversely, when you are trying to fade a shot, to meet opposite conditions of wind or slope or pin placement, the toe of the clubhead is blocked from passing the heel, and this hand action, or lack of it, is accompanied by a proportionately open stance. I may be repeating this until we're both purple in the face, but only because I find hand action so gallingly and so universally misunderstood. Believe me, you will not be able to finish this book and still misunderstand it.

I admit there's some danger in trying to be too tricky about hooking and slicing on purpose. But even so, the average player has a better chance of hitting his shots straight after he learns how to curve them. If he doesn't understand what produces the variations, his chances of preventing them are slight.

The eight, seven, six, and five irons become less and less versatile as the face becomes straighter and straighter. Each iron also calls for a slight adjustment in the address position. You move the ball about a half inch farther forward for each straighter-faced club, and your head that much farther back. This distributes the weight more evenly and, as the clubs get longer, makes the arc of the swing both wider and slightly flatter. The degree of pinch is minimized also.

A full nine iron, to me, means a shot of between a hundred and and a hundred-and-ten yards long. For the major professionals, this is light hitting. But it is still longer than the average. A hundred-and-twenty yards—with no wind—means either a slugged nine iron or a comfortable eight iron, and I much prefer the latter. It's nice to say you've reached such and such a hole with an extremely short iron. But if you did so with the wind at your back, and by lobbing the ball so high that it didn't stop when it hit the green, you've sacrificed considerable control. *And remember that these higher irons are primarily control clubs. It is never wise to force them.*

The range of the seven iron, for me is a hundred-and-twenty-five to a hundred-and-thirty-five yards, the six, 135-150; and the five, 150-165. As the clubface becomes straighter, you hit down on the ball less. Because of different styles—punching versus swinging—certain players have always been able to play certain clubs best. A short, firm puncher is usually better with the medium or short irons. The swingers seem to play the straight-faced clubs better. Yet there are exceptions to this. Snead, for example, is a master with the medium irons, and equally at home with the long ones. I am a swinger, certainly, but I have always felt a relative advantage from the five-through-the-nine iron and wedge.

Perhaps you tend to slight your medium irons during practice sessions. They are not, to be sure, such spectacular shots as the long irons into far-away greens. But if you neglect them you are making a mistake, for they are more immediately rewarding. A good medium iron shot will leave you a short putt. An equally good long iron can't be expected to get you that close. So, if I had to choose between a practice session on the long irons and some work on the five-to-nine irons, I would take the latter choice. They pay-off better.

CHAPTER 11

THE LONG IRONS

THE long irons are the most demanding clubs in golf. In the first place, their proper execution depends heavily on power, for which there is no substitute. Sufficient clubhead speed is absolutely necessary to get the shot high enough to be useful. The Sneads and Palmers, Littlers and Hogans can hit the ball with such force. From a normal fairway lie they can use even the one iron and still get the ball up and away powerfully.

I myself only feel confident and strong enough with the four iron. As a matter of fact, because of its combination of power and versatility I prefer it to any other club. Step me down to the three iron, however, and I immediately feel doubts about what I can bring off, especially if the wind is behind me and the lie is not too good. I simply can't mash the ball against the air with enough force for a reasonable range of effects.

Let's return briefly to the muscle-strengthening exercises of our first chapter. There's no plainer case for their need than with these straight-faced clubs. In the days of unlimited clubs I carried the one and two irons. But I used them almost exclusively on par-three holes which had trouble everywhere except in front, so I could tee the ball up, and freeze it low on line. Even after passage of the fourteen-club rule, I occasionally left the seven iron out of the bag to carry the two iron for just such shots. But from cuppy fairway lies, or with the wind strongly behind me, more clubhead velocity is needed than I can supply with a two iron. I have never had the power to make the ball plane well enough consistently. In addition to the physical strain, there is the mental aspect, too. I am even less likely to make the free, full swing which is essential for the shot.

The five wood, on the other hand, has been a steady, faithful friend, for just these situations. With it the shot can be wafted high enough and far enough without undue effort, and stops just as quickly when it hits, anyway. You can't have everything, of course, and against a very strong wind the five wood with its higher trajectory is not as effective as the two iron. But I still stay with it. And I have never felt too handicapped by my lack of siege-gun power for the long irons. If I could borrow greater strength for just one department of play, I wouldn't use it here, but on the drive.

Furthermore, between me and the ordinary golfer there is something of this same difference in power-quotient. I would imagine that the average man and most women find the four iron about as tough to hit straightaway as the three iron is for me. So I have long advocated a set of clubs for general use made up of six woods, six irons (the four iron the straightest-faced), a wedge, and a putter. It doesn't seem fair to saddle the greater percentage of golfers with clubs only a few can use well, but obviously my powers of persuasion leave something to be desired. Six woods can be ordered specially, but still aren't included in any standard sets that I know of.

And lack of power isn't the only stumbling block with these long irons either. For, although the arc of the swing is longer than that used for shorter irons, a larger and more precise portion of the ball must be caught on the clubface to obtain even passable results. The radius of the American golf ball is eighty-four-one-hundredths of an inch. If it sits on an ideal lie and you have a nine iron in your hand, you can strike anywhere in an area of eighty-three-one-hundredths of an inch with a descending blow and make a respectable shot. Admittedly, if you hit the top half of the ball, you'll top it with any club. But contact fractionally below center on a downward trend will make the ball run up the face of a nine iron and fly out well. Not so with the two iron. You have to get almost all of the blade under the ball and just miss tipping the grass to bring your result up to standard. With the margin for error less, your basic fundamentals have to be more meticulously put into play.

The first of these fundamentals naturally is the grip. The left hand "V" points diagonally across the body to the right shoulder. The last three fingers of the left hand must hold on very securely. Don't allow them to become loose at the top of the swing. You must pay particular attention to getting the right hand "V" straight up and down, or at least pointing no farther right than the right eye. For if you're going to have both these "V"'s pointing at the right shoulder you will have to be unusually tall or unusually strong to get long irons to fly off the turf as they should.

The stance is important, too. You must avoid setting your feet too far apart. Keep them a little closer together than the width of your shoulders, to facilitate your pivot. A full, supple body turn is necessary; you should get the right hip out of the way going back with almost as much freedom as for a full drive. Such a turn will keep the flexibility and softness in the swing needed to get the ball up well. This flexibility in the hands helps you develop clubhead speed without hitting so hard with the arms and shoulders that you get out of position. But remember: flexibility is not sloppiness. You must still grip tightly enough to keep the club from slipping around in your hands.

The ball should be played farther forward, closer to the left heel than for the medium irons. If you have it back too far toward the center of the stance, the shot is pinched too much to get up properly. Thus two-and-a-half or three inches inside the left heel is about right for a three iron, with the head held only fractionally in front of the ball's position. The shot is nearly a lob, but not quite. The bottom of the arc comes just slightly in front of the ball, and the faintest trace of pinch is imparted, to make sure the clubhead doesn't catch the ground first.

At the top of a swing, with a square stance, your left hip should be pointing approximately at the ball. (Fig. 20). This hip then starts the downswing, more emphatically and vigorously than for the shorter irons, but still without pulling the head and shoulders off the ball. At impact the left hip is slightly more forward than it was in the address position. Through the force of its downward pull, and under the stress it puts on your back there is particular danger of your head moving as well. Thus stiffer-trunked players sometimes play the ball a bit more forward to help them stay over the ball for shots where maximum body torque is used to develop full power. At impact, the left shoulder is a little higher, too, than at address; the right shoulder, a bit lower. The hands and arms go through with their full flailing action to finish high and flexibly. Of necessity, since these are longer clubs, the swing will be on a slightly flatter plane. If at the very top of the follow-through the club were dropped, it would touch the player just off the left shoulder, whereas with a nine iron it would drop to the curve of the neck.

As I've said before, with these straight-faced clubs your choice of shots is more limited. You cannot ordinarily hit them with half or three-quarter swings unless a strong wind is in your face, or unless you can tee the ball up on a par three. Long irons are easier to fade than to hook. For a shot of a hundred and sixty-five or seventy yards, with negligible wind conditions, I feel perfectly comfortable slicing a three iron. But if I have to go five or ten yards farther, I do not usually try to hook it. Instead, I bunt the five wood.

The essential factor in long iron success is to keep the swing long and loose. With less weight in the clubhead, however, and with less confidence in the result, this becomes doubly difficult to do if I feel I must force the shot. So I have to stay well within myself. Trying to hit too hard tightens up the muscles and restricts rather than increases your power. The shot becomes more punched, with less of the necessary loft. That is why, by and large, swingers like Snead, Littler, Nelson, Hogan, Armour and Shute hit the long irons best. It is said that nobody who hits these

THE LONG IRONS

FIG. 20

shots well can be a poor striker of the ball generally; whereas, someone who masters the short irons may be. I agree.

But even superlative swingers have trouble with the long irons from time to time. Bobby Jones, for instance, relatively late in his career when I was mature enough to study his game closely, was still hitting the medium irons beautifully, and the fairway woods just as well. But I never saw him hit a really good long iron. This was apparently the first part of his game to suffer from lack of top-flight competition and work.

As far as I'm concerned, the long irons are most dependable on the par-three holes, where they can be teed up and do not have to be forced. However, I would rather hit a four or five wood easily than *slug* the irons, even off a tee. But if I can merely exert my normal effort, the long irons can help me, too, especially in windy conditions. The straighter face, and the more upright, stiffer shaft make for better directional control. And, of course, off the tee the wooden peg guarantees the height I need on the shot.

To sum up, in playing long irons the swing must be *flexible and soft*. A stiff, punching action, with hands prominently leading the clubhead, keeps the ball too low for any but the most powerful hitter. My old boss, Craig Wood, was such an exponent. He could tear into the ball so hard with stiff wrists that it still got up, though at impact it was practically submerged. And even he, for all his effectiveness in playing into the wind, had trouble in wet weather.

Now a square or slightly open stance will help you get the ball up. The hands lead the clubhead microscopically. The weight is more evenly balanced. If we had a scale under each foot they would register nearly the same at impact.

The variations are more limited, as we have already said, because of the difficulty of hooking the ball with a straight-faced club and getting it sufficiently airborne. However, if the wind happens to be against you strongly enough and the lie good enough to raise the shot well with a hook, the technique is still the same. The right foot is drawn back a bit to aim you slightly to the right of the target, so that the hands can move the toe of the clubface past the heel faster in the hitting area.

In the straight shot, the toe passes the heel, but more gradually. In the fade, it does not go by at all. And to match and allow for each of these gradations in hand action a correspondingly different stance is called for.

However, sooner or later all teachers have some pupil rush up to them with a photograph of a top star, showing him in a follow-through with the club-shaft horizontal and the toe even with, or still below, the heel. "See," the pupil will shake his head. "Where's the evidence of wrist action there?"

The only answer is to take the picture in context. The star was purposely trying to cut the ball and thus blocked out his hand action. There's a very famous and widely used picture of Tommy Armour in just this attitude, when he was actually trying to fade the ball.

But if he had been trying to hit the shot straight, his usual finish would show the toe directly above the heel, even in a three-quarter follow-through. There are ample photographs of Armour making this more characteristic swing.

Among present-day golfers Gene Littler in my opinion is the finest long iron player. He's even better than Armour or Nelson or Cooper or Shute in their prime. He takes a divot with these clubs, but a very shallow one. And the ball sits as lightly on the green when it hits as the average player's does when hit with a medium iron. That remarkable little fellow, Jerry Barber, also gets the ball up well, though he's not quite as straight as Littler. Palmer is good, partly because of his greater strength. I have never seen Nicklaus up close, except in pictures a magazine sent me to analyze. I was thoroughly impressed by them.

Let those of us below this front rank admit, then, that even if long irons are the mark of a good powerful swing, we are still not going to be stubborn about wearing ourselves out trying to hit them. They are the glamor shots. There's no doubt about it. Fortunately you and I can avoid them when we have to by substituting the five or four wood. When we come to those shots which seem to be between clubs—longer than a three iron, for example, but shorter than a five wood—choking up on the five wood gets the ball adequately high, while cutting down a bit on its distance.

I would like to be more positive. But there's no sense batting your head against a stone wall, especially if you can scramble over it instead. Much as I hate giving in to limitations which need not exist, I still feel you have to recognize those that do.

CHAPTER 12

THE FAIRWAY WOODS

THE old adage about driving for fun and putting for money is true. But I include fairway woods in the fun category, too. There is a great thrill in picking the ball cleanly and powerfully from the fairway and in watching it go sailing away into the distance. I get more credit than I deserve for being expert with these woods, simply because I use them oftener than more powerful hitters do.

But in the days when I employed a definite lateral sway, I was not a precise striker of the ball from the fairway itself. At least not in the same class with Harry Cooper or Bobby Jones—especially as watered fairways came into vogue making the ball harder to get to cleanly. On the long par-threes, however, I really did more than hold my own because then I could tee up the ball. Finally, after abandoning the lateral sway in the 1940's, I became better from the fairway, too. Now I get a good portion of power into those shots.

By far the leading criterion of fairway wood play is stability and precision of head position. The ball must be hit *exactly* at the bottom of the arc, not on the way down, and not on the way up, unless the lie is unusually bad in one case, or unusually good in the other. To do so consistently your head *must* be anchored, with *the back arching strongly to hold you in place.* Cooper and Jones did this uniformly well, but I think the best illustrator of its importance was Lawson Little.

Little was an extremely fine player of fairway woods, often using the driver and getting his shot away high and powerfully—when by all rights he shouldn't have been able to do so at all. For he had a bad gripping habit which shut the face, and I was continuously amazed at how he got the ball up. In the address position he would put his right hand on the club perfectly. But then just before starting back he would regrip with his right hand sliding the "V" back to a point over his right shoulder. Yet he kept his head so beautifully in place coming into the ball by arching his back and using his strong leg muscles that in spite of having the clubface several degrees too closed, he was nevertheless able to get the ball up. This knack, of keeping the bottom of the arc right at the ball, without wavering off it in the hitting area while applying full power, is the secret of success with fairway woods.

Bobby Jones himself hit the most remarkable single shot I have ever seen in golf, and did so with a fairway wood. I was paired with him in the first round of the first Masters tournament ever played, in 1934, and as we came to the 495-yard 11th (now 2nd) hole he was left with a two-hundred-and-forty-yard second shot off a downhill lie to a green about a hundred feet long but only about fifty feet deep. The pin was placed to the right, behind a strategic bunker. I hit as good a two-wood second shot as I could. After a long roll it came to rest just off the left hand edge of the green, leaving me with nearly a ninety-foot chip to the pin instead of the more delicate shot across the bunker which would be hard to stop on those slick greens. I felt contented enough, with a good chance for a birdie on the hole, and I turned to watch Jones.

His somewhat longer drive had stopped below the crest of the hill, on a fifteen degree downslope in the fairway. As he addressed the ball with his left foot well below his right I saw he was aiming directly for the flag—with a four wood. I assumed from the lie he wanted to drop the ball in front of the bunker for the shorter pitch across it. He took one of his characteristically full and graceful, rubbery-looking swings, and the ball got away powerfully and high considering the steepness of his lie. But then it seemed as if he had miscalculated and that the shot would carry into the trap on the fly. When, instead, it flew all the way over this trap— a carry of two hundred-and-forty yards—with a slight fade, I waited for it to bounce over the green. Instead it bit like an eight iron, and stopped about seven feet beyond the hole. I was flabbergasted. I called out to him, "Could I see that club? I never saw a four wood go that far in my life."

He smiled and showed me his two wood.

From that pronounced downhill lie he used a straight-faced club, got the ball up powerfully, and hit it so lightly on a slick green that it stopped after a ten-foot roll. The flexibility of his swing, and the knack of having the very bottom of its arc come right at the ball, gave Jones his mastery.

I myself holed-out a three wood once on the 430-yard ninth hole at Midlothian in an invitation tournament honoring Walter Hagen. But probably the most famous fairway wood shot of all was Sarazen's double-eagle two on the 520-yard fifteenth hole at Augusta in the 1935 Masters. It enabled him to tie and later beat Craig Wood in the play-off. I happened to be leaving that very green just ahead of Gene. I saw his ball hit above the creek bank and, instead of falling back into the water, it kicked up on the green and bounced right along into the hole. It was an instance of good luck rather than good execution. The shot flew too low for any assurance of carrying the creek, and that two was really one fortunate kick away from being a six. Since then, however, I've read that Gene's lie was not good, that he had to toe-in a four wood and hope. This accounts for the low trajectory.

The fairway woods normally should be pure lobs, with the bottom of the arc coinciding exactly with the back of the ball. You may have to pinch the shot if the ball is in a fairway depression. And if it is sitting high on a tuft of grass you may be able to take a driver and hit it slightly on the upswing. But these instances are the exception, not the rule.

Ben Hogan, to be sure, used to hit all his fairway woods, good lie or not, with a noticeable pinch. Yet this particular shot was not one of his strong points, in my opinion. Playing with Byron Nelson, as he often did, he might be ten or fifteen yards ahead on his drive, only to be caught by Nelson on the second shots. For Nelson nipped the ball perfectly off the turf, right at this correct bottom point of the arc, in spite of a ducking action of his head on the backswing, and a sort of rocking recovery as he came into the ball. Therefore, to pinch these shots unnecessarily is a waste of power.

The gripping, of course, is still the same. The left hand "V" points at the right shoulder, the right hand "V" points at the nose, with pressure diminishing from the last three fingers of the left hand to the thumb and index finger of the right. This leaves the right forearm without the tension which would impede its flexibility going back or its throw or triggering action in the hitting area coming through.

The ball is placed well forward of center, but not quite so far forward as the left foot. As a general rule it is about an inch and a half inside the left heel, although in progressing from the two wood to the five wood you may move its position a bit more toward the center of the stance. The weight is evenly balanced, and the head is exactly opposite the back-side of the ball. (Fig. 21).

For the two wood, which has only twelve degrees of loft, the ball must be kept as far forward as possible without moving the bottom of the swing's arc behind it. An inch inside the left heel is about right. The shaft of this club, being fractionally longer than the others, makes you stand a bit farther away from the ball and thus put the swing naturally on a flatter plane. *Keping your head still is imperative.* If it does move forward on the downswing, under the stress of the hit, you either take loft off the face, which you can't afford, or push the shot violently to the right, which is just as bad.

The more supple player can play the ball a little farther back. With his greater flexibility of trunk, a strong exertion of legs and hips to create power will still not pull him off the ball.

A stocky player, on the other hand, like Gene Sarazen, whose

FIG. 21

feet and hips have a tendency to swivel under the force of a heavy, or too heavy, hit, must move the ball's position farther forward. The recent televised eighteen-hole match between Sarazen and Henry Cotton at St. Andrews illustrated the difference between Gene's good swings and his bad ones. He himself corrected the latter. To win, with a fine performance on the back nine, he cut down on the force with which he pulled at the ball with his left hip and side. The extra force had been causing him to move off the ball, or swivel to the left.

I have seen Jimmy Demaret, too, normally a very graceful swinger, hit so hard at the ball with his body that a photograph showed his left ankle completely turned over on the follow-through like an awkward skater. So you see nobody is immune from trying to create too much power. The harder you pull with your body and hips the stronger and more flexible your back must be to hold you in place over the ball. I don't say you shouldn't experiment to find where this point of maximum torsion is, just short of pulling the head laterally. But when you find it and the chips are down, for heaven's sake stay within that maximum.

The arms should hang down comfortably just outside a vertical drop from the shoulders, to give freedom of arm motion. There should be no friction of the upper arms with the body. The clubhead itself is placed carefully behind the ball, with the center fractionally inside the center of the ball to allow for the slight inside-to-out path in striking it. The feet are close enough together to permit the body to turn freely, but not so close that you will lose your balance.

To help you start away from the ball smoothly, and to relax tension, the waggle and the forward press may both be helpful. It is a personal matter, really. Some particular preliminary motions help one player; others help another. But the criterion for any of them is whether they help start the swing rhythmically. By moving the hands forward gently and turning the right hip toward the ball (much as you rock a car one way to help push it the other) many people can begin the body turn away from the ball more smoothly. The forward press doesn't guarantee this, however. I have only the tiniest hint of it in my own swing. It should be used only if it helps you begin a smooth pivot and backswing.

In this backswing the body turns approximately ninety degrees, but the head must stay in a carefully steady position.

The heavier, more bull-shouldered, or more tense-bodied person may find this full ninety degree pivot beyond him, without pulling his head laterally off the ball. Fortunately because of his compact build, such a person can usually develop enough clubhead speed from a lesser pivot.

The point is to wind yourself up as fully as you can without moving the head itself, the hub or focus of the whole swing.

The older golfer must keep his full pivot. He actually needs it more than his younger opponent; and here again we come to the necessity for exercises that keep the muscles stretched out and flexible.

I differ sharply with many of my brother professionals in this regard. Many of them say that as we get older we must settle for shorter, more compact swings, with less body turn, even if such swings result in less power. Proficiency, they argue, should be gained through greater control of the shorter shots, and the chips and putts.

But, though I concede that the one and two irons are beyond my present powers to handle adequately from the fairway, I certainly don't accept this general point of view about settling for shorter distance on all your shots, particularly the longer ones. So keep your full pivot, even if you have to work a little harder, practice a little longer, and take a few more exercises to retain it through suppleness of body and muscle. These exercises are not time-consuming and their rewards are great.

My wife, Joan, accuses me of vanity in this respect. But I am turning more freely now, coming into the ball with stronger hand action, and thus hitting the ball farther than I ever have in my life. If I come home to dinner announcing some new distance mark for a drive on a particular hole, she is still not impressed. "You used to beat them by being straighter," she says. "And by chipping and putting their eyes out. For heaven's sake stop bragging about being a big hitter." She would be right if I did neglect these other aspects, or if gaining ground in one direction meant losing it in another. But that's not really the case.

And it is deeply and truly satisfying to see that, barring serious illness or physical difficulties, the inevitable decline of power can be held at bay, not by working yourself into a lather and straining your heart, but simply by keeping your muscles stretched and flexible. They then do gratifying work for you in preserving your vigor and your delight in this game. Until Bobby Jones' back laid him low, for example, he kept his power through his full pivot and willowy action, as Mac Smith did, and lately, as Byron Nelson and Dutch Harrison have done. *So retain your pivot to hold onto your power.*

Now, to return to the swing itself: when the turn going back is completed you should find your forearms a little above shoulder height, on a plane in keeping with the ball's position outside the feet. After your wrists cock fully, the club should be about parallel with the ground. For the swinger, the shaft might dip a bit below horizontal; for the puncher it might stop a bit short.

Each player's pivot and the cock of his wrists should then *be to the particular limit for him, short of moving his head or letting the club slip in his hands.* (Fig. 22).

As your left hip reverses its turn and starts down toward the ball your wrists are still cocking going back. The two-way stretch in the left arm and side can be felt as the club is pulled down and the wrist cock retained. When the shaft reaches belt level again, or just below, on its way toward the ball, the hands become the main agents of a forceful hit. Up to this point, they have been impassive; now they release the clubhead with a spring-like effect which through momentum carries the player up and around again ninety degrees past the point of impact, still on a plane roughly comparable to that of the backswing.

After impact, the head is finally free to move forward and up, since the ball is away and gone. But one telltale indicator of the better players is that little or no such motion takes place, even

FIG. 22

after the hit. Sam Snead's head position after a full follow-through is remarkably close to where it was throughout the swing. Though his body is fairly thick-set, and though he is more than fifty years old, he is still pliable enough to maintain this central focus all the way through.

A far more ordinary habit is to let the head come up and the posture straighten in the follow-through. But even if this straightening and moving forward of the spine does occur well after the hit, there is an insidious tendency for it to creep farther and farther back into the swing, to come earlier and earlier until soon part of the movement is actually occuring in the hitting area itself. Then the player is at a loss to explain his suddenly erratic golf, not realizing how close he has been to it, even with his good shots, for a long time. Holding this head position from beginning to end of the swing—for all the stress it puts on the hip and back—is far and away the best prescription for holding it steady in the hitting area until the ball is actually off the club.

I have seen Ben Hogan's final head position six or seven inches from the point it held until the ball was hit. And if any of this motion started before the ball was well away it probably accounted for his tendency to pinch some shots, even the drive itself, too much. On these occasions the ball would skim the entire length of the tee, like a plane leaving an aircraft carrier, sometimes just ticking the grass before it finally arose. The gallery would ooh and aah at the planing effect, but the result would be a drive of two-twenty or thirty instead of two-sixty, so I don't think Ben intended it.

I have already mentioned how one exemplary striker of the ball, Byron Nelson, could get his fine results with a perceptible trace of vertical head motion, and there are others, like Art Wall and Jerry Barber, who share my tendency to move over the ball. But any such motion multiplies your timing difficulties, makes practice far more necessary to control the tendency to sway. Somehow it is the kind of fault that grows and grows with time and it is best to scotch it while you can.

And right here with these fairway woods the whole theory

crystallizes into reality. Head position simply makes or breaks these shots. Nine times out of ten the fault will be caused by head motion if the woods start going wrong.

You might be interested now in learning how far my fairway shots travel. Remember I am a somewhat shorter hitter than the star pros but a good deal longer than the ordinary golfer. My two wood is good for about 220 or 225 yards, if I catch the ball flush and well. The three wood reaches anywhere from 210 to 220; the four wood, from 200 to 210; and the five wood about 190 to 200. These are not prodigious distances, but I think it is foolish to risk accuracy by trying to hit these clubs too far.

The technique with all of them is nearly the same. The ball may be moved slightly more forward as the club becomes more straight-faced, but only slightly.

I certainly don't like to pinch these shots: too much distance is lost. But at the same time it is better to pinch them than to hit behind them, since all but the two wood have enough loft to get the ball up even when struck a descending blow. Remember: a perfectly hit fairway wood is a lob; but making the bottom of the arc occur at precisely the back of the ball is so intricate to manage that it is probably better to make sure your errors come on the side of pinching rather than digging, if they must come at all.

However, there is only one shot that goes any farther, or gives you a more exhilarating feeling when well hit. We will take up that shot next.

CHAPTER 13

THE DRIVE

RECENTLY, I heard a gentleman from Phoenix talking woefully about what had happened to his drive. He had played golf, he said, from the age of eight or nine. When he was that young a certain tree on one of the holes always caught the best drive he could make. He remembers the great thrill of carrying over that tree one day. Soon he was doing it without worry or strain. In time, the tree all but vanished from his consciousness—until recently. "Do you know, Paul," he said ruefully, "I'm beginning to see that tree once more from that tee. I'm coming back to it. It's going to get me again."

I sincerely hope it doesn't. As a matter of fact a major incentive of this book is to forestall that decline. Understanding the fundamentals and using exercises to make them more effective should definitely help. I don't want to give my wife's complaint too many grounds for being true. But as I go over courses today which I remember having played in the past, it would not be human if I didn't notice I am reaching particular spots I was short of ten years ago. For any tiger you've got in you will come out in this long part of the game. In comparison with the average touring professional I am still relatively short off the tee. This does not bother me, because I am hitting the ball better, and in golf your own performance and its improvement must always be your own criterion. It does not trouble me to be out-hit by thirty-five or forty yards (which was the tabulated margin, incidentally, in my 1938 match with Snead, and not a hundred yards, as you often hear), if I feel I am hitting the ball well for my standard. It does trouble me if I feel I am not hitting the ball up to that standard.

This second most important of golf's two terminals has immediate effect, both physically and psychologically. There have been very fine golfers whose striking of the ball has been excellent except at the two ends: driving and putting. Dick Metz particularly comes to mind. If his putting and driving had been as good, relatively, as his fairway woods, his long irons, and his medium irons, his many near-misses would have been wins. Why he couldn't extend this mastery of the intermediary phases to both ends always puzzled me.

In my own case, during the nineteen thirties, I think my driving was a little underrated because of my lack of conspicuous power. In a few tournaments where every drive of every player was measured, mine averaged two hundred and thirty-one yards. (Now, however, I am at least ten yards longer than that.) This was dangerously near not being long enough to reach the tough par-fours. I certainly could not afford to lose even five yards and still have anywhere near the same chance. But with my average drive I was still within range of most of the holes I had to get to.

Furthermore, I did have control, and this is a factor that cannot be overlooked even in the premium power shot. I rate Sam Snead as the greatest driver who ever lived, because he combines unusual power with unusual accuracy.

Craig Wood I rate number two, with Bobby Jones and Byron Nelson not far behind. Harry Cooper would be right up there with them, if accuracy alone were considered. In the same seventy-two holes where my drives were measured, Wood's averaged 258 yards in one, and 263 in the other (Snead was in only one of these tests and his average was 273). Chick Harbert, on any individual drive, could hit the ball out there, too, but not on average and too often not on line. Ben Hogan hit the ball very powerfully, but on the whole more erratically. George Bayer is, without question, the longest driver of them all, but his accuracy, too, has to be improved before he can be ranked with Snead.

Bobby Jones was an authentic master of the drive, and it is too bad more of golf's growing audience have not seen him play. For he had a unique, change of pace to his swing; he suited his length off the tee to the particular hole he happened to be playing. He would hit his drive 235 or 245 on the shorter par fours, a little longer for the medium-length holes of 400 to 420 yards, and then really whack it out there 265 or 270 for the 460-yard hole, or for a par five he felt he could reach in two. He did this apparently without greater effort; he simply took the club a bit farther back each time, turning a bit more and widening the arc. But he never seemed to hurry the swing or change its tempo. It was a beautiful thing to watch. The only player I ever saw who managed anything like this distance-versatility was Macdonald Smith.

In the early part of my own career Jimmy Thompson was the king of swat, and I remember him staging an exhibition at an early Masters tournament that I have never seen equalled before or since. He stood there on the practice tee at Augusta and started off with the nine iron. Each pitch shot would bounce just in front of the caddy, to be taken easily on the first hop. I watched Jimmy move the caddy back and begin hitting the longer irons with the same result. The boy never had to move. Each shot landed right at his feet. When finally Jimmy repeated this process on three-hundred-yard drives I was sure nobody had ever hit a ball as far or as straight. These long powerful shots never obliged the caddy to move more than a step to the left or right to retrieve them. It was a breathtaking performance. The practice was sustained; Thompson kept at it a full half hour, without making a crooked shot. Followed then by what might well be called a shocker on the golf course.

As you might guess, after Jimmy finished this truly fabulous warm-up he went to the first tee for the first round of the tournament accompanied by a large gallery. He promptly knocked his first drive so wildly that before coming to rest it crossed three fairways: the first, the ninth, the eighth, and it finally settled in the rough on the other side. He made this awkward swing and flying hook immediately after the most magnificent practice session I have ever seen a player stage in my life. The moral is this: anything can happen to your nerves once that whistle blows and the pencil goes to work recording all that you do.

In driving, finding the proper tool for your individual needs is supremely important. We'll discuss the matter in detail in the chapter on equipment, taking up swing weight and shaft stiffness and so on. Here, I just want to mention the shape of the driver. The stronger player will get his best power and control from what is called a two-way bulger, meaning that from heel to toe the face is curved (with anywhere from six to nine degrees of arc) as well as from top to sole. The two-way bulger makes the head of the club produce greatest compression at the very center or thickest part of the ball where it is most alive. With a flatter clubface the compression is more dispersed.

The principle of getting greatest impact through the deepest part of the ball is like the carpenter using a ballpeen hammer to drive a big nail or spike with the least strokes, as opposed to the flat-headed hammer he uses for a tack or more slender nail which he doesn't want to risk bending. It's another example in golf—like the high-compression ball—of the rich getting richer, or the powerful more powerful. Because they can naturally produce more compression, the big hitters are able to use advanced equipment which increases that compression—equipment denied the light hitter, who actually needs it more. Thus the average player has to settle for less of this two-way bulger and more loft to get the ball up. Still it is a most important element in design for power in the number-one wood, and how much of it you, personally, can use is worth some experiment.

The swing for the drive must be the most powerful you can make consistent with control. If to hit one drive two hundred and forty yards you are willing to accept getting only two hundred and ten on another, you will not be as well off from a scoring standpoint as if you hit them both two hundred and twenty-five, since you won't be able to select where the variations occur. Steadiness and reliability of power is what you must have. This again, is the source of Snead's superiority.

The grip remains the same, of course. The ball is placed immediately opposite the inside of the left foot, (Fig. 23) in the case of the average golfer, or slightly inside that point for the taller or more loose-jointed person. The stance normally is a bit closed, which encourages you to move the bottom of the arc an inch or two behind the ball where it should be.

For the drive should be hit on the upswing. It took me a long time to grasp all the technical, scientific reasons for this, but from my first days as a twelve-year-old caddy at Hot Springs, Arkansas, I compared the results of one kind of trajectory with the other.

I'd stand down the fairway about a hundred and fifty yards out from the tee and watch the balls come toward me. Often the ultimately shorter shot would seem to start out more powerfully, low and hard. Sometimes I could even hear it whizzing through the air, which would seem to be a sign of power. But then it would gradually hang like a stalling airplane and fall almost straight down to the ground with hardly any roll.

Another type of shot would start off a little higher, but would then reach out in an arc like a rainbow, with each end of its trajectory quite similar. When it struck the ground it would apparently leap forward faster than it went through the air. This was an optical illusion to the viewer, caused by the ball changing direction like a putt dying toward the hole which hits the lip and seems to go faster sideways. What has really changed is the angle of vision.

But my other observations were sound enough. There was no whizzing sound with the longer shot. Scientists say that air friction is on the under-front side of the ball when a larger amount of back spin is produced, and this is the sound I heard from the weaker efforts. Backspin also causes the ball to rise more steeply, though starting lower, and then drop straighter down without roll. The drive that is struck on the upswing has no top-spin, but it does have a minimum of backspin. So its descent is more gradual.

Use the wooden tee, then, to do what it is made for, to help you hit *up* on the ball. Tee it high enough and far enough forward so

FIG. 23

that you strike up on it past the bottom of the arc, producing this rainbow-like trajectory with its greater run. (Actually you get the most distance from four hundred revolutions a minute backward, hit up in the air at a forty-five degree angle.) Ted Williams, one of the greatest baseball hitters of all time, has said that for maximum carry he always tried to hit up on any pitch that was below the belt. Certainly the golf ball would fit into that classification. Arnold Palmer, too, I am told, is teeing his ball a little higher nowadays to hit his drives more on the upswing. As a result, he is getting more power, which he doesn't need, and more accuracy, which he does need.

The feet are placed farther apart for the drive than for any other shot, but they should still not be so far apart that the pivot is restricted. Body turn is not only a source of power, but on the backswing it actually starts you rhythmically away from the ball. After you have put your hands on the club correctly and placed your feet properly in the slightest closed stance, the first motion should be a turning of the right hip away from the ball.

There are plenty of equivalents, anatomically speaking, such as the left hip or shoulder turning toward the ball, or the left knee breaking inwardly, or the right leg bracing. They all go together and I don't care which you say happens first. People do, however, seem to simplify the process of taking a full pivot if they concentrate on making just one of these motions. So pick the one that works best for you to produce the start of a full turn.

When the body has turned far enough to cause the arms to move, the shaft starts backward on its proper plane, transmitting this motion finally to the clubhead. It all happens in such close order that the observer probably sees no such distinctions. Yet the right sequence in which to produce the backswing is a winding up of the body which makes the clubhead move last. The player is then on his way to a full turn.

If he goes about it by prying the clubhead away from the ball with his hands first, with less body motion following, he does considerable violence both to the proper swing plane and to the coordination of clubface position with body turn. And this, as we have pointed out earlier, is intricately meshed even for shots as short as the pitches. With the more limber-trunked player, or with women generally, or even with the supple-wristed, lightly-muscled man like myself, this drag of the body, arms, and hands away from the ball (ahead of the clubhead) will be more noticeable than with the stocky person like Sarazen or Palmer whose backswing is truly more one-piece.

Nevertheless the motivating power in taking the club away from the ball is body turn, whether subjectively initiated by the feet, knees, hips or shoulders. And this turn to the right should continue until the body has reached about a ninety degree position from its starting point.

Now the clubface, turning more or less in unison with the body, will have also opened ninety degrees, on a plane which if extended would intersect the ball (or at least be parallel to a line drawn from a suspension point between the shoulders to the ball). (Fig. 24).

Here is a much discussed and fought over crossroads in golf. Players catch innocent bystanders and ask them to look for a moment at this artificially stopped top-of-the-swing station, to see what has happened to the clubface going back. And well they might. For it is true that whatever they do going back they must reverse coming down, though not at the same points.

In my own terminology the face is still square if it is parallel to that swing plane which we have described above. It is closed if its plane, extended, would pass above or outside the ball.

Usually this closed position signifies that on his way back the player has held the clubface at right angles to the ball for some time, while the body has been turning away, so that even though the face is square to the ball it is closed with relation to the body. Or, if you prefer, you can say the clubface has opened to a lesser degree than the body has turned.

You can also, by independent hand action in the other direction, open the face more than the body turns. Then, at the top of the swing the club face's plane, extended, would strike some point well inside the ball, or between it and the player's feet.

110 THE DRIVE

FIG. 24

So this top of the swing position is a checkpoint, to see what has happened, if you're in any doubt about it. My own term, "square," means to me square to the body, as it was in the address position, and not square to the ball after the ninety-degree turn has taken place. You do run the risk of jabbering at yourself and others if you delve deeply into this matter, but all the same it is fascinating. And how in the world will you ever hold your own in locker-room arguments if you don't learn a little of the terminology?

It is a most technical argument, I admit, but I think we ought to risk it. I don't propose to exhaust all meanings which different teachers give the terms "open," "shut," or "square."

But there is certainly one well-known school, presided over by Claude Harmon, one of the country's best-known professionals, which advocates keeping the club face square *to the ball* throughout the backswing. I thoroughly question whether most of them—Harmon himself, for that matter—actually do this all the way. But those who come nearest achieving it—like Doug Ford—do reach a more shut-face position at the top of the swing than I do. The clubface is practically horizontal, its plane extending well outside the ball. The left wrist is in line with the forearm, or in what is called the dead-hand position, forced there by the hands holding the clubface closed to the ball as the body turns away going back.

But the really important point is what has to happen on the way down. Obviously, the hands cannot trigger the clubhead from a position of ninety degrees to the ball, and then through it again to another ninety degrees past. They are already square to it at the top of the swing. Such hand action would smother or drive the ball into the ground. Instead, the clubhead must be dragged through with the arms.

To swing it fast enough, then, or to maintain enough speed, the player must have the arms and shoulders of a blacksmith to hit the ball far enough without the crucial turning action of the hands which the rest of us depend on. He must also work his hips and spine very fast to make sure they get through well ahead of the clubhead and keep it from closing on him. That is why, I truly believe, so much serious back and hip trouble plague practitioners of this school, especially as they get older. Moreover, for the rank and file, it simply is not a powerful enough way of striking the ball. I know from experiment that I have all I can do to hit a drive more than two hundred yards in such a fashion, and it would wear me out to do that very often.

By my dissent against this method, I do not mean to detract in any way from Doug Ford or his record, which is one of the most consistent in golf. Beyond that, I admire without qualification the bull-dog way he goes at the game. I am merely saying that this closed-face or shut-faced technique (which is also sometimes called square, but square to the ball, remember, not square to the body) does not seem widely adaptable to me—least of all to older players, or to those without natural power to burn.

So your hands and arms should turn in unison with the body. I do not open or close the clubface by any conscious manipulation of the hands. Often this independent turning of the wrists one way or the other, intentional or not, can be traced to the grip.

Having the hands back, or extremely to the right, for example, can mean that as the club is taken away from the ball the clubface is turned under, or to the left. This is caused by natural muscular tension asserting itself when the hands become passive, as they should become, in the backswing.

Conversely, if both "V's" were pointing at the left shoulder, the hands might revert to a more neutral position going back and open the face more than the body turns.

At the top of the swing the back of the player is just about facing the target. In the process of pivoting, the spine, which was comfortably bent over at address, must hold its position. While the hips turn on a nearly horizontal axis, and the shoulders midway between horizontal and vertical, your spine acts as a suspension point for both turns. The face of the player remains fixed upon a spot about two inches behind the ball.

If the body has turned ninety degrees, the arms have swung back upon an inclined plane. If we tied one end of a string around your neck, the other end to a wooden tee which we inserted under the ball, and then drew the string taut, it would represent the plane the club should be swung on. When the arms are swung back on this plane to the top of the swing they have traveled through an arc of nearly a hundred-and-eighty degrees from their vertical starting point.

The wrists, continuing to cock after the arms have stopped, then carry the clubshaft to its full arc of two hundred and seventy degrees—slightly more, perhaps, for the swinger, slightly less for the puncher.

By the time the club has reached this maximum point the body has started uncoiling the other way, back toward the ball. The tension created in the thigh muscles of the right leg and the deltoid muscle of the left side through the full stretch of the backswing begins to subside to allow for a turning of the body back to its starting position. Though this return pivot of the body back to its address position is completed very quickly, it leaves the arms and hands only about half-to-three-quarters of the way through their downswing.

Somewhere about now, at the half or three-quarter point down (a little earlier with the weak-handed person, a little later with the strong-handed one), the wrists come into play. They begin to uncock, to make their throw or thrust or turn (however you wish to think of it) in order to get out of the path of the fast-moving clubhead.

There is impressive evidence, from high-speed camera studies, that strong, quick, free-wheeling wrist action does not actually speed up the clubhead, as most of us have always thought. Instead, the wrists actually keep the clubhead from decelerating in the hitting area from the maximum speed reached when the shaft of the club is horizontal.

Yet this unleashing of the hands is still a major factor in clubhead speed, whether creating or maintaining it. For, while the hands are making their throw, the turning action of the body and the speed of the arms is arrested. Neither comes to an abrupt stop. But there is a pause. The motion of the body seems to die out as the player comes to the ball. The clubhead is flying so fast through flexible hand action, that, of course, it cannot be seen. And the momentary pause of body and arm thrust at this point which all topnotch swingers seem to have gives the illusion of effortlessness. "He hits the ball so easy," they say, watching a swing like Snead's. The effort and speed are all there, but they are invisible to the naked eye.

What can be seen (the arms and shoulders and body generally), does not appear to be moving as fast nor working as hard in a good swing as in a bad one. A poor swing lacks the unleashing, unseen, hand action which enables the body to be relatively quiet. The high handicapper is leaning on the ball more, trying to push it out there with his arms and shoulders, and his attempt to do so shows. At best arms and shoulders are very poor substitutes, and the visible difference in form that the two kinds of swings demonstrate can often be quickly appreciated even by the most untutored observer. One looks graceful; the other does not.

But people can also come to the wrong conclusion about what they have just seen. If without the trigger of hand action the high handicapper merely keeps his body quieter in the hitting area he may not hit the ball even as well as he does now. He has to put the cart before the horse, in other words. It is not the body turn stopping, but the hands hitting, that separates the good golfer from the bad one. Indeed, it is the hands hitting that actually slows down the body and arms. To the novice golfer this is the awesome mystery of power. For it is all so invisible. Consequently he is likely to pick out something he can see to explain it: a digging action of the foot, or some personal peculiarity of body action or positioning.

At the time the clubface begins to compress the ball at impact, the hands are also back at their address position. But they are not locked there. They are alive and turning. The left wrist is turning over in a backhanded motion (supination) and the right wrist is taking a forehanded motion (pronation). They continue to turn through until the shaft of the club is horizontal again, past the ball, with the club's momentum carrying the body around to the

THE DRIVE 115

finish on a plane comparable to the backswing.

So the drive's success, from the combined standpoint of power and accuracy, depends jointly upon the clubhead speed generated and the ability to maintain that speed through the hitting area. When I was at Annandale, Professor Tom Cape made some thorough tests of these dynamics by means of a high-speed camera. It had already shown him secrets of what happened to metals under stress, and he wanted to see what it would show about a golf swing. His research is only in the early stage, and I hope he goes on from there. But he took a wide sampling of swings from four very different golfers: the outstanding Betty Hicks, woman professional; Mike Austin, one of the longest-hitting pros in the Los Angeles district; a slightly better than average medium handicapper from Annandale; and myself.

In all these swings—professional and amateur, woman and men alike—the clubhead was moving fastest at the horizontal point of the downswing. In the case of Betty Hicks, it was traveling ninety miles an hour. After she had struck the ball, and after the shaft had reached horizontal again on the follow-through, her clubhead was going eighty-eight miles an hour. This spoke very well of her ability to maintain clubhead velocity. To keep this high percentage of clubhead speed through the hitting area and beyond, she managed a very rapid turn of the toe of the club from a trailing position with relation to the heel to a leading position. Her driver, incidentally, was C-9 in swing weight (which we'll discuss later)—relatively light for men, relatively heavy for women. She got an average of 217 yards on forty balls.

When it came to my turn, I was then using a heavier club than I now use, with a more limber shaft—a mistake which I've since corrected. But the camera showed my swing moving the clubhead at ninety-five miles an hour at the first horizontal position, and ninety-one miles an hour on the second, or a loss of four miles an hour. I had an average of 238 yards from forty balls.

Mike Austin's club, moving a hundred and twenty-six miles an hour on the first horizontal point, was going a hundred and twenty-one at the second, or a loss of five miles an hour, at a greater speed. He had an average of 281 yards.

But it was the amateur who really showed us something. His club was actually traveling faster than Miss Hicks's and faster than mine at that first horizontal point. Yet he barely got within twenty yards of her, and was forty yards short of me. From a speed of ninety-seven miles an hour at the first horizontal point, his clubhead slowed down to fifty-six miles an hour at the second. With this deceleration his average drive was only a hundred and ninety-seven yards long. He was not slicing, either, but going straight, with a driver of D-3 swing weight, which was exactly the same as Mike Austin's.

On the basis of these studies we conclude that the main determinant of transmitted power is not just the maximum clubhead speed a player can produce, but also his ability to *maintain* that speed through the ball. Austin, of course, was longer than anybody, because he got the club going faster to begin with, but not only because of that. The percentage of speed he retained was also about as large as that of anybody else. But the amateur, however, was shorter than either Miss Hicks or myself because he couldn't keep the clubhead going once he started it, so as to make it hold its speed. And the reason was that in the hitting area the toe of his club did not move rapidly by the heel. This was not a matter of strength, but of quickness and flexibility. The toe of the club was moving, or trying to move, but very awkwardly, because of the stiff, labored action of the man's wrists.

I know of no more graphic illustration of the importance of hand action. Furthermore, I think that most golfers who take up the game later in life or who do not play often, sadly neglect this unseen, vital element of powerful, consistent play. Thus the usual fault—you might say it runs as high as ninety percent—is going past the ball with the body, before the hands have had a chance to help or make the clubhead catch up. Head position and maintenance here is very important, too. If the head stays an inch or two behind the ball, all these other actions have a far better chance of occuring on schedule. If the head tends to wander forward, opposite the ball or even in front of it, you hit the ball a descending blow which robs you of its carry and its roll, and probably of its proper direction as well.

So by all means, cultivate maximum hand action for the drive. It is the real thrill shot of golf. I know that when I hit the farthest the chances are that I am also hitting straightest, because I am turning more freely and getting my hands into the ball more flexibly. I suggest you keep track of the places on your course which you normally drive to. There is always a challenge to get past them the next time—on the *fairway*, not in the *rough*.

Finally, do not be upset by somebody else driving his ball past yours. Stick to your own guns, and forget him, whether he's shorter or longer. There have been some curious episodes in head-to-head duels among great drivers. Somebody like Thompson, for example, could not play with Snead without knocking the ball all over the course trying to out-hit him. On the other hand Snead himself, reputedly so impressionable, could handle other long drivers, like Hogan or Harbert, without ever allowing them to alter his own game.

I wouldn't be so honest, though, if I didn't say that on some courses, especially in California, it gives me a pain or two to see some big sprayer in the wrong fairway reaching a green with a five iron, while I am hitting a drive and a five wood straight down the middle. I even begrudge the long driver some of his advantage at places like Augusta. If his drive is crooked he can often curve his second shots out from under trees where there is no rough. And in three out of four cases, if he carries the ball two hundred and thirty-five yards, he hits a downslope which runs it on much farther. The light hitter's drive, carrying two twenty, hits the face of the hill and immediately stops.

I don't require that the odds be three to one for me, I just require that they are not that much against me. And there are plenty of courses—Pinehurst, Medinah, Los Angeles North and a host of others—where, if I am beaten by the big driver, I don't begrudge him his triumph for a moment. On these courses the big man must be straight and long, not just long, so more power to him. When I go home, afterwards, I simply go back to my exercises.

CHAPTER 14

ODD LIES

IN playing golf it has always been a source of pleasure to me to figure out an angle the other fellow has overlooked. For this sort of extra sleuthing is the smaller man's opportunity to neutralize his opponent's greater power—or at least to compete without the issue being decided beforehand. I can thank my lucky stars that out of necessity I got a grounding in the finer points of the game. Because, in addition to having to learn them in order to develop a good amount of golf wisdom, I still find them fascinating. Any light hitter who is successful must have a little more of this savvy than the husky fellows. So I will tell you about some of the unusual shots I have learned to make over the years when I found myself in tough spots. Perhaps they will help you too one of these days.

One such odd shot was a cut shot across a bank from the backside rough of the fourth green at a Masters championship, when I was paired with Lawson Little. The pin was in such a difficult position from where I stood that I decided to play beyond it, to hit a rise past the flag with a semi-cut, semi-explosion shot which might spin back. If the ball hit anywhere short of the flag no shot in the world would have stopped within twenty feet. It was bound to end up on the lower terrace. But my alternative came off, the ball spinning back to within close putting distance.

The most prominent area for using your wisdom lies in the unusual, the untoward shot where the ball is not sitting on a wooden peg, or in the middle of the fairway, but has unpredictably found trouble. If you are better than your opponent in getting out of trouble, you will start catching up to him. For I assure you, nobody, even the best striker of the ball who ever lived, plays down the pipe line all the time. Get familiar with your trouble shots then, so they don't scare you by their novelty.

The straightforward uphill and downhill lies are the simplest and easiest to solve. But observation still convinces me that few players really adjust properly to the fact that the ground has been tilted on them. From a horizontal lie the golfer naturally keeps himself vertical to the ball in his address position. Yet if his ball is on a slope, he has a tendency to resist that slope with his stance, instead of conforming to it in such a way that he is at right angles to it on this lie, too. Whether the slope is level, or goes up or down, you must retain your ninety degree relationship to the ball in order to hit it properly. If a slope is three degrees downhill, for example, the body must be tilted three degrees forward. If, instead, you bend your right leg to keep yourself at right angles to the horizon, you drastically reduce your chances of making a solid hit. Nine times out of ten your club will catch the ground behind the ball first, and bounce into it for a thoroughly topped shot. The odds against you are the same as if you had tilted yourself backward three degrees when the lie was level.

Of course, when you lean the body three degrees forward in such a case, to preserve your ninety-degree angle to the terrain, the face of your club now has less loft on it, with relation to the horizon, and this also has a psychological effect sometimes. It makes you lean back to scoop the shot. This is the very worst thing you can do. You simply must concede that the ball is going to fly as many degrees lower as the body has leaned forward.

But there is a limit to how far forward you can lean. Even though you lean forward one degree to bring yourself at right angles to a one-degree slope, and two degrees for a two-degree slope, and so on, if the hill finally becomes too steep—and in my experience this is at about fifteen degrees—you are tilted too far forward to maintain your balance throughout the swing. You then must lean back a bit on the right leg, to keep from falling down. But when you do so you must also move the ball further back toward the right foot.

I've rigged my example to three degrees purposely, because that is about the difference in loft between one club and the next one. From a hypothetical downslope of three degrees, then, if I desire two-wood trajectory I have to take the three wood, to offset the loft removed by the hill. Similarly, if on a six or eight-degree downslope I want two-wood trajectory, I have to take the four or five wood. Even in these cases, with my weight leaned proportionately forward to keep at right angles to the slope, I will not quite get two-wood distance with the shots. A club with eighteen or twenty degrees of loft on it—and a slightly shorter shaft, to boot—cannot give the ball two-wood compression. But it still gives better distance to meet the ball solidly with a four or five wood, while maintaining a ninety-degree address angle, than to move the ball back toward the right foot, shortening the club to do so.

There is another way, however, of adding loft to a downhill shot. By fading it you can get even a two wood off a three degree downslope to fly at normal height, if the contours of the fairway permit the ball to drift right. But I would rather see the average player try to hit the ball straight from any lie where balance is hard to maintain.

So remember: on a downhill slope, keep your body at right angles to the hill. Use a club with enough loft to compensate for the down grade. And try to convince yourself that you are making a level swing from the attitude you take.

For uphill lies you must do just the reverse. On a three-degree upslope your weight moves back on the right leg by that much, to hold yourself at right angles to the terrain. A two wood would then hit the ball with three-wood height; a driver would have two-wood loft. The only time you would vary the address position (and this holds true for going downhill as well) would be in the case of a bad lie. If the ball were in a hole, or in a cuppy fairway lie, you would move it back toward the right foot. Moving it back in this way might complicate your loft problems. But you would not change the body's posture with relation to the ground, at least not within fifteen degrees of slope. However, if the lie is both very steep and very bad, you go to the irons.

I realize there is another theory about how to play downhill shots. Many teachers say the ball should always be moved back toward the right foot. And, indeed, this will work. My objection is that it obliges you to shorten your grip on the club and this markedly depletes your power. If you're within short iron distance of the green this choking-up on the club doesn't hurt you, but for the wooden clubs or longer irons I prefer my own method of making sure the body stays at right angles to the slope. I can then play the ball at its normal place in the stance.

The uphill lie, of course, should be much easier, since loft is added to the face of the club. But most players still do not get their stance properly angled to the lay of the land. In this case they should lean their weight back. If they don't the clubhead will not swing parallel to the ground at impact, but will go rather sharply into the face of the hill. The shot usually gets away fairly well, anyway, because of the uphill slope. But the excessive pinch causes loss of power on the long shots and lower trajectory and more run on the shorter shots than the player expects.

At La Jolla, we climb steeply up to the eighteenth green at about a nine or ten-degree upslope. And to see how prevalent this habit is of hitting too much into the hill instead of up it, just walk down and look at the divots. Especially on the short iron pitches this sort of landscaping (caused by leaning the weight too much on the left foot to counteract the slope, instead of adapting the stance to it) means loss of considerable control. The player should take a straighter-faced club, lean his weight back, and try to swing as though his stance were level. This will give him the right kind of trajectory and stopping action for his shot. Finally, just as off a downhill lie, if you position yourself properly, the tendency is to let the weight slide forward and produce a fade, so the law of gravity tends to pull you backwards on an uphill lie and make you hook or pull the shot. It is best, therefore, to allow a margin for these probabilities.

Coming now to the sidehill lies, the ball above your feet should not be too difficult to hit correctly if two warnings are kept in mind. Number one is to realize that from this sort of lie, with the ball above your feet near the position in which a batter hits a baseball, it is actually closer to your suspension point between the shoulders. So you must either move farther away from it than usual or grip well down the shaft of your club. I favor a combination of the two; both choking up a little, and moving a bit farther away from the ball to flatten the swing plane. The weight should also be kept well back on the heels to accommodate this flatter plane.

A second factor of this shot ought to be more obvious than it apparently is. For, if on a moderately steep sidehill lie with the ball above your feet, you look down at the face of a rather lofted iron, you will see this loft turned not in the direction of the hole at all, but considerably to the left (provided that you are right handed). And the more loft on your club, the farther left it will be aimed. It is simply not presenting itself straight upward as it does on a level lie.

In ratio to the amount of loft and the amount of slope, therefore, you must adjust for the ball going left, either by taking a slightly straighter-faced club and opening it in accordance with the steepness of the lie, or by aiming well to the right of your target so that in flight the ball hooks or pulls back toward it. I prefer the former system unless the pin is to the left of the green. Then I would want the ball to approach by curving and bouncing to the left as it hits.

If, however, the shot should go in straight, and if it is about six-iron distance off a lie with the ball well above my feet, I will take the five-iron and open the face at address, proportionately to the slope. The shot will then go around six-iron height, and will not hook or pull.

A fade from such a lie, if the situation calls for it, is extremely difficult to execute. With the same six-iron distance to go, I would then probably drop down to the four iron, lay the face back and make sure I cut the ball by dragging the clubhead through heel first. The chances are that even with these provisions I would get only a trace of left-to-right spin. I'd feel I'd accomplished something, though, if I could manage even this small amount accurately.

Probably of all the lies commonly met, those where the ball is below the feet give the most trouble. If you stand in a normal way for such a shot, as though the lie were level, the neck of your club will be almost parallel to the ground and the toe will be sticking well up in the air. If you strike the ball with the clubhead in such an attitude, and if you are somehow successful in getting the blade on the ball, its heel hitting the ground will cause the toe to turn in, twisting the club out of your hands and hitting the ball sharply to the left.

But the ball is supposed to go right, you say, from such a lie. And it will, if you sole the blade level with the slope. This attitude brings the shaft up to a nearly vertical point, and makes you stand much closer to the ball. It also aims the loft on the club to the right. With the swing plane much more upright as well, you are certainly going to push or fade the shot unless you do something to counteract conditions forced upon you. Furthermore, in this upright position, with the ball closer to your feet, you are most likely to produce the shank—usually because the club is taken back too far inside for the upright plane this particular address position demands. Just as when the ball is above your feet you are more likely to hit it on the toe of the club, so with it below your feet are you more likely to hit it in the heel. Unfortunately, the latter error is far more costly, and it also makes you feel as though you have lost your reflexes or have come unglued.

Therefore, from this lie, with the ball below your feet, more caution is called for. You make the opposite adjustments of clubface position to allow for the opposite effects. You even overdo these adjustments a little: you toe the face in not only to keep the loft from pointing to the right, but also to allow for the tendency of your more upright swing to fade the ball. Thus the face is aiming quite a bit to the left—enough, at any rate, to keep all the fade out of the shot. If you are within eight-iron distance of the green, you take the nine iron and toe it in. The same procedure is used with the longer irons and woods. But it is always unwise to try to get too much power from this sort of lie. The pivot is more restricted, your balance more precarious, and solid contact with the ball a bit more difficult. Be conservative, then, and simply try to meet the ball well.

These, then, are the four main types of odd lies and these are the particular rules for solving them. (1) Take more loft for the downhill shot, (2) less for the uphill one. (3) Take less loft with the ball above your feet, and open the clubface. (4) Take more loft with the ball below your feet, and toe the club in.

There are, of course, countless other predicaments awaiting you in this crazy game. In spite of all the beautifully manicured courses we have these days, a ball still seeks the lowest point it can find in any fairway or in any rough. And, as we have said before, if it does run into any depression or divot hole, or end up with some obstruction like a rock or a tree root behind it, you must make sure to position yourself over it so that you hit the ball first, and not the ground or obstruction behind it.

You do this by moving your suspension point much farther forward than usual, the particular degree forward depending upon the particular steepness of arc required to get the clubhead cleanly over whatever is behind, and at the same time hit under the ball. The closer or the higher the impediment is, the farther forward the head must be placed. Moving the head forward, however, robs your shot of loft. So if I have to play from a deep divot mark, or from any place with a high spot immediately behind the ball, I cut the shot to add to the loft. Thus we come again to the pinch-cut, which we've mentioned before. I allow for the drift it produces directionally, and for its partial loss of power. And I make absolutely certain that the hands never allow the toe of the clubhead to catch up to, or pass, the ball as I hit it.

There is one instance, even on a good level lie, when an extremely forward head position is still called for. Say, for example, that your ball is lying cleanly, but only a foot or two short of some tree trunk which your club would wrap around after a full swing. Instead of chipping it out weakly for the loss of a stroke, you can use this bad lie procedure to stop the clubhead from hitting the tree even after a fairly full swing. If I had seven-iron distance to go from such a spot, I'd use an eight iron and move in front of the ball to hit the ground on the downswing so abruptly that all forward motion of the clubhead would stop an inch or two after the ball was hit. The shot would fly much lower, of course. Too straight-faced a club could not be used. Probably the four iron would be the limit.

Under such circumstances, a wood is not a good idea, either. The broad sole makes it too likely to skid or bounce off the earth into the tree trunk, instead of digging into the ground short of it. I have seen hardy souls, however, free to swing back as far as they liked, but with no room for the follow-through, attempt to use the two wood and purposely cost themselves the club. It takes plenty of mental discipline to execute a powerful swing under such conditions, knowing you are going to break the shaft in two or bark your hands and arms just after you meet the ball. Yet not flinching is the only way you will ever bring it off. For that matter, *not flinching is the major rule in all trouble shots*, even those involving less risk.

I remember the volatile Clayton Haefner once, in the Beaumont Open, having to meet just such a problem. The fairways of that course were lined with huge trees. You knew it was only a matter of time before you were going to get behind one. Even I accepted the inevitable fate, though usually on such a track I'd bet myself against the field.

At any rate, Clayton finally found himself stymied by a tree. Not, however, until he had put together two pretty good rounds. In that tournament they also conducted a fairly large calcutta, and one little lady who bought Clayton was following him around feeling very good about her prospects. He was either in the lead or very close to it as he came up to that tree midway through his third round. The obstruction was much the same kind as the theoretical one we've just discussed, except that there was also a very thick root sticking up behind his ball. In making his swing Clayton didn't position his head far enough forward to steepen the arc over this root. The clubhead hit the thick, heavily gnarled wood, glanced sharply off, and bounded entirely over the ball without touching it. Haefner was left slightly off balance by this unexpected collision and complete miss. His right foot crossed in front of him, and as it did so he kept right on walking. Those who knew him well knew that he was on his way into the clubhouse, leaving the ball behind him exactly where it lay. Nothing in the world was going to stop him. But the little lady took longer to react. Eventually it dawned on her that her purchase was on his way out of town, and quickly coming to life she ran after him. "Please, Mr. Haefner," she cried, "please come back. You'll hit it the next time." Her pleas, alas, went unanswered.

I myself have missed a ball in a situation similar to that, by miscalculating the path my downswing would take. My error caused the clubhead to bounce off a boundary stake behind me and go cleanly over the ball. In the same way, tree limbs catch a club on the way down and completely spoil your shot, by the tiniest deflection, it seems. That is why it is always a good idea to go through the arc slowly before hitting to see where your swing plane will take you—extending your arms, though, as you would actually do under the stress of swinging. Neglecting to do this is the usual cause of failure. Many people think that if, in testing where your swing will go and what it will hit, you touch a leaf or limb or fence you automatically cost yourself a stroke. This is not so. You are penalized only if this preliminary swing knocks down or moves any part of the obstruction.

Playing away from fences is not nearly as hard as people think it is, either. Assuming you are right-handed, and the fence is to your right, the ball can be close against it and still be perfectly hittable. You must toe the club in enough to point at your target (sometimes this can even be almost behind you). You then swing back and through on a line parallel to the fence. The toed-in position of the blade makes the ball go sharply left, though its much lower flight restricts your distance with the straight-faced clubs.

Even a fence on the left should not be a hopeless case, or one where only a chop with the left-handed putter will get you free. If the toe of a lofted iron is turned upside down and swung left handed along the barrier, its loft will aim and knock the ball back to the right a pretty good distance. To hit the ball that way is not as hard as it seems.

After the four basic slopes, and the obstacles, trees and fences, there is still the rough to deal with. In California, its absence or sparseness as compared to the Eastern variety, is a great handicap to the development of a well-rounded golf game. Southwestern players going East for the first time usually feel like writing their Congressmen about what appear to be severe penalties for driving off-line. Lo and behold, they can't hit the same easy shots to greens from out of the rough. They feel cheated. Even the normal bent-grass fairways (where the ball sits much lower than in the Bermuda grass they are used to) look and act more like rough to them. The Eastern-variety golfer, with the head start of solving more varied problems of lie and trajectory, comes West without this handicap. However, he probably feels a little frustrated by not being able to put his greater golf wisdom to use out here.

Even for native Southern Californians, however, there is one tough shot out of the rough which must be learned: alongside greens where artificial watering makes the grass grow longer and thicker. I learned this game in all the lush Southeastern setting of grass and trees and snug fairways. But it was at Brentwood in a Western Open of the late Forties that I first discovered how to get better results from this sort of devilishly-delicate lie. I mentioned it first in the bunker chapter, because that same "V"-shaped arc must be used.

However, I'd like to repeat some of the features of this special type of swing which was invented by Dutch Harrison, the old Arkansas traveler. He certainly got out of that spinach consistently better than anybody else in the tournament. The rest of us often flew the ball so hard from the heavy grass right at greenside that, with no backspin possible, it ran across to the same trouble on the other side. Or, in trying to avoid this, we didn't move the clubhead solidly enough to get the ball to the green at all. We were sometimes taking four to get down. Three was common, and two a rarity. Dutch never left the ball too short or hit it too long. He always seemed to get down in three from there and frequently two. It was time to find out why, so I watched.

His swing looked extremely long for the distance of the shot. But it was also extremely slow, like an underwater or slow-motion swing. The real secret was that he was taking an iron grip. Moving slowly through the grass, but heavily and firmly, the clubhead neither flipped the ball too quickly nor failed to make consistent contact. The ball was practically lifted, or shovelled out. I started trying this slow, labored, but very tightly-gripped stroke, and found it helped me greatly. I now breathe easier hitting second shots, too, into greens guarded by such heavy grass. Missing these greens by a couple of feet no longer inevitably means at least three more to get down.

Hitting longer shots from thick rough, unfortunately, is mainly a matter of brute force. Very heavy grass usually demands an iron. Closely-knit strands will twist around the wood and deflect it. If the mat is not too thick, however, a lofted wood is actually better. It spreads the grass instead of cutting or chopping it like an iron.

But the texture and consistency of particular roughs take particular knowledge. In a recent British Open a strange, thin-looking fuzz seemed to invite fairway woods. However, invisible wires quickly dragged the ball down into the rough again. Sometimes the only way to avoid this was by playing directly back onto the fairway.

In conclusion, I would like to urge you to take the right attitude toward these shots that are off the beaten track. Instead of regarding them as evidence of a bad golf game (which should be dispatched quickly before anyone finds out what you have done) bone up on these trouble shots thoroughly and figure them out with care. Realize that everyone gets into these toils, and that if you know how to recover better, with less soaring of temperature and score, you have given yourself the same relative advantage as if you'd sunk a long putt or hit a better iron shot to the green. Pride goeth before a fall, and if somebody's got to go down, let it be the other fellow.

CHAPTER 15

EQUIPMENT

I'VE heard it said that a good carpenter with poor tools can do a better job than a poor carpenter with good tools, and that may be true. But applying this theory to the great variety and range of golf merchandise available, I see no reason for any golfer—good, bad or indifferent—to use equipment which is either inferior or unsuited to him personally. Of course, the abundant supply calls for careful selection. This chapter is included to help the reader find his way through all the equipment available, make an intelligent choice for his own needs and save him hundreds of dollars in the process.

At the outset though, let me say that reading it is not going to mean you can walk into any pro shop and outfit yourself with clubs of the proper weight, proper design, proper shaft stiffness for your particular makeup, or even find a ball with the perfect compression for you. Trial and error is the only way to make sure, and probably even then there will be plenty of room for doubt. I've been at this game for over forty years, and I still experiment constantly.

The golf professional, in this respect, has a relationship to the golf manufacturer comparable to that of the race-car driver to the automobile maker. We're supposed to try out all the crackpot gadgets we can think of to improve performance. If ninety percent of them are never put into general use by the average golfer because they don't work well enough, that trial and error is still largely responsible for the great progress made in all types of golf equipment. The major breakthrough came around 1930 to 1933. Since then, most improvement has been made in uniformity of manufacture. But we have also learned much more than we used to know about swing weight, shaft stiffness, and so on. My own recent experiments have not been so much with these factors—where I agree pivotal discoveries have been made—as much as with different kinds of new materials.

One hypothetical case mentioned in the driving chapter bears directly on this matter of club selection. If a person hits two drives totalling four hundred and fifty yards, is he better off having one go 240 and the other 210, or having both go 225? The latter was declared clearly preferable. But it is a continuing question for every golfer with all types of equipment: whether to take clubs or balls which demand his very best effort to produce good results, meaning a marked falling-off with poorer tries, or to take those which reduce the extremes. I think you always have to break the answers down specifically.

If a person is swinging in such a way as to produce two hundred and twenty-five yards of power, he should use a club of average weight and average shaft stiffness. On the other hand, if he can produce average power of two hundred and forty yards, he should have a club of somewhat stiffer shafting to bring about a comparable amount of accuracy. The more limber shaft at the higher speed will be too distorted for reliability. I'm talking not only about directional accuracy, but about trajectory control, too. The latter is almost equally important. With the iron shots still another control factor, backspin, is affected by shaft stiffness.

In the early days of my golfing career, I used very flexibly shafted wooden clubs, and medium-shafted irons—successfully enough as a relatively light hitter to feel that I was on the right track with my selections. But then I had the opportunity to talk with Admiral Tom Brandon, who had just become a designer with Spalding. He explained to me why he thought a lot of my half-topped shots were not due so much to any fundamental fault of execution, as to the type of equipment I was using. He said the shaft was too light, for the weight of my club and the power with which I swung it, even though my power did not equal that of the big hitters. The combination of soft shaft, heavy clubhead and the power I did have was distorting the shaft to such a point that the ball could be slightly mis-hit even when I did not commit a fundamental error in striking it. If I added any such fundamental mistake to this built-in variable, I was in real trouble. And like any other golfer I was, of course, bound to make such mistakes.

This distortion, Brandon concluded, was especially costly with the straight-faced fairway woods. The shaft was so limber it would not spring back in line fast enough to return all the loft at impact. So the backward bend and turn of the face under was causing the ball to fly too low. I certainly did hit an unusual amount of shots that didn't get up as I wanted them to, particularly after courses became better groomed and watered and the ball lay deeper in the lusher grass. As a result, I began to test the stiffer shafts Brandon recommended.

The first day I tried them out I immediately decided that if I had to play this game with that kind of equipment I'd give up golf entirely. The new woods felt like boards, and I did not enjoy them. But I began changing my tune when I noticed that the ball was getting up more uniformly. At first I still thought I wasn't getting equal distance after the change-over. (And maybe with the more flexible shaft I had hit a few harder blows that went unusually far for me. Yet by the same token whenever I did mis-hit one it had been very short.) Now at least I was getting better trajectory and more uniformity of distance.

Then I made another change, this time in clubhead weight. When I had gone to the stiffer (and therefore heavier) shaft, while still keeping the same weight in the clubhead, the "swing weight" (which is a calibration of the energy factor in swinging the head of the club, to match one club with the other) had dropped from the very heavy E-2 I had previously used to about D-6, or D-7. Now I began dropping the swing weight farther by lightening the clubhead, down to the present, where I am using a driver of about D-1. There has been a continuous gain of distance in this process, but I won't want to go hog-wild about it and say that if I went farther down into the middle C's of swing weight I'd be even longer.

Other factors enter into my improvement—chiefly, I am sure, the exercises I have been doing to strengthen my hands and arms. As these have enabled me to swing the clubhead faster, I have been able to lighten it and take more advantage of the greater speed.

But all of this is a tricky business. The scientists tell us energy equals mass times velocity squared. Thus if you double the mass and retain the speed you double the power, while if you double the speed and retain the mass you quadruple the power. That is why they urge us to use lighter clubs with stiffer shafts, that can be swung faster than heavy, whip-shafted ones.

I personally think, however, that they overlook one all-too-human condition: every golfer has a limit to his reflexes, some point-of-no-return, past which even lightening the club will not increase its speed. At that point he may be able to move a medium-light club as fast as a very light one, and the greater weight will give him added power.

Weight should be retained, in other words, where additional lightening of the club does not produce more speed. And the individual must locate that point for himself, without succumbing wholly to the mania for very light clubs. He can only find this optimum balance of speed-versus-weight by extensive trial and error. But unless he knows what he's experimenting for he can't even do that.

So much for the abstract reasons why more experts are—and probably more general golfers should be—using stiffer-shafted, lighter clubs. What yardsticks are there, besides work, for fitting the right weight and stiffness to the right player?

The manufacturers have come up with an impressive array of different designations to help us. As a representative of one of them I am going to stick here to those particular terms with which

I am thoroughly familiar. But I do so not for any endorsement of that line. I want this chapter to be a completely academic discusion related to value, not a commercial for any one product.

In these designations an "S" shaft means stiff, though there can also be different shades of stiffness within the class itself, up to the point where "X" is used to denote maximum stiffness. "R" is medium. And "A" is light. In addition, there are "L" shafts and "LL" shafts, the first for the lady of average power, and the second for the lighter-hitting gal. The "A" shaft then would be very firm for a lady, and light for a man. The "R" is medium for a man.

Even these different degrees of limberness vary, as I have said, within each classification. The usual procedure is to put those with about the same variation together in a set of clubs. You may ask, "Shouldn't the spoon be a bit stiffer than the two wood, and the two wood a bit stiffer than the driver?" The answer is yes. But by cutting the shaft of each descending club fractionally shorter it is also made fractionally stiffer.

There are other compositions on shafts besides steel, of course, and we ought to say something about them. I find the pure glass shaft too limber for all but the very lightest hitter. Its shaft, like hickory, does absorb shock, because of the greater torsion that steel cuts down. The glass shaft encasing a steel core, on the other-hand, is as good as any other shaft, though not necessarily better. Like the pure glass shaft, however, its durability is not equal to steel.

All right. Now let us say that the good male golfer, with a general knowledge of the variety of clubs he can choose from, hits the ball between 225 and 250 yards and asks which of them he should use. His average drive may not be that long, but he is capable of this distance if he catches the ball well even without the help of wind or unusual roll from baked-out fairways. He, in my opinion, should use an "S" shaft in his woods and an "X" shaft in his irons. With the irons he is after reasonable power, but primarily he wants maximum control in direction, trajectory and spin. With the driver, on the other hand, he wants reasonable control with maximum distance.

This man should also be using a swing weight of C-9, at the very lightest, to D-3, at the heaviest. The stronger, faster handed he is, the lighter the swing weight. But lengths of shafts also vary, and every additional inch means eight more swing weight points (there are ten within each letter)—a bit more than eight for a heavy-headed club, a bit less than eight for a light-headed one. So I really don't think I can margin my recommendations any tighter without closely observing the speed reflexes of this particular golfer.

The young star from California, Phil Rodgers, whom I've watched since he was fifteen, gets good distance and direction out of an even lighter driver of C-6 swing weight. At the risk of quibbling, I think this is a little too light for him: that he is getting his distance through too much speed and too little mass, so that his control suffers a bit. I'd like to see Phil bring the swing weight up to C-8 or C-9.

On the other hand, I can think of many people who are getting too little power, although they are enjoying excellent control, by using clubs that are too heavy and rob them of a lashing hand action.

As far as the dead-weight is concerned (or total weight of the club, as opposed to swing weight), I can generalize even less. Stiffer shafts necessitate heavier clubheads if the swing weight is kept the same, which then produces more over-all weight. Thus a stiff shaft of about D-0 swing weight usually means a club of about 13¾ ounces. To get the same swing weight with an "R" shaft, that is somewhat lighter itself, the clubhead must be lighter, too, giving a total weight of perhaps 13½ ounces or a bit less.

Personally I place far more faith in swing weights than I do in dead-weights. The latter is more of an indication of the components in the club, than it is of their distribution. So the best procedure is to decide first what kind of shaft you need. Then see what swing weight with that shaft gives you the best combination of power and control. Let the dead-weight follow those leads.

In the early days we selected by dead-weight alone. It was our only way of differentiating one club from the other. We handled different degrees of flexibility by simply paring down the hickory shafts until they gave the whip we wanted. We found this greater flexibility made the club feel heavier to swing, even though it was lighter in total weight. Here, the concept of swing weight was born. The scientists took it from there, telling us that when we lightened the shaft of the club we lowered the point of percussion. After that they worked out the scale we now use.

But let's get back to specific cases. Our first example of the 225-250 yard hitter, was actually of a rare bird.

The player who hits his good drive somewhat shorter, in the 200-225 range, is in a minority, too, though a larger one. He should be using a light "S" shaft, in his woods, with the same swing weight as the longer hitter, reducing the over-all weight, and firm "S" shafts in his irons, within the same swing-weight range.

Down one more notch, those hitters getting between 175-200 yards from their good drives make up the largest segment of male golfers in the world. Most of us are pretty egotistical about how far we hit, and hate to admit falling into lower categories. We also sometimes tend to figure our distance on burned-out fairways. Actually 175-200 hitters make up fifty percent of all golfers. And generally the "R" shafted woods, with the same swing weight, about D-0 or D-1, serves them best. And light "S" shafted irons. The dead-weight again is thus made a little less. With progression in power, of course, such players might move up to a stiffer shaft and, therefore, slightly heavier club.

Finally, just as markets rarely label even the smallest eggs "small" (but "medium," "medium large," etc.), so no one by choice puts himself into the lightest-hitting class. But those players who knock their good drives from 150-175 yards are in the second largest group numerically. The light "R" or even the "A" shaft, with about C-8 swing weight should suit them. This reduction in over-all weight to maintain the swing weight makes the club very light. And here we may be getting into another one of

EQUIPMENT

those cases where, since the player obviously does not have fast or clever hands, a heavier swing weight, increasing the amount of mass, would be better. Lacking suppleness of hand action, this light hitter may still be strong enough to swing the club at the same speed and so gain a little distance. (See Chart 186-A)

Best Drive goes:	225-250	200-225	175-200	150-175	less than 150
Shaft Stiffness: Woods	S to heavy S	S or firm R	R	A	L or LL
Irons	Heavy S or X	S	Light S or R	Light R or A	A or L
Swing Weight: Woods	D to D-5	C-9 to D-2	C-8 to D-1	C-6 to C-8	C to C-5
Irons	D to D-5	C-9 to D-2	C-8 to D-1	C-6 to C-8	C to C-5

Coming to head design for wooden clubs—depth, loft, and curve—the striking power of the player strongly influences the soaring effect he can give the ball, and also critically determines the dimensions of club he should have. If he can hit the ball hard enough to produce this soaring action, he will get it up with the straightest-faced driver, or one of about eight-degree loft. If he cannot do this (and the 175-200 yard hitter cannot: there isn't enough friction of air against the ball at lower speeds), he has to have about ten degrees of loft to bat the ball up for him. The average lady's driver should have about 12 degrees.

The strongest hitter's driver should also have the two-way bulger we've previously mentioned, with an arc of no more than nine degrees from heel to toe, and one of no more than six degrees from top to sole, diminishing then down into the fairway woods. When this somewhat rounded face hits the round ball it gets all its force through the middle, or thickest part, while the flatter face distributes its blow more hemispherically over the whole surface.

The depth of the driver's clubface is related to power, too, for the harder you hit the ball the wider it distends, so that you need more clubface to get all of the ball on it if you don't hit dead center every time. A compression producing 250 yards, distends the ball to the size of a half dollar on the clubhead. So if you place a half dollar in the center of the face of the driver a little margin should be left at the top and bottom for safety.

The fairway woods should be shallower. With them there is more chance of the ball protruding under the club, since those shots are harder for us to get down to. The shallower head then goes through the middle of the ball, anyway, and helps get the shot up. But you still don't want the face so thin that from a good turfy lie you are likely to cut under and sky the ball.

The driver's depth for the stronger player, then, is about one-and-a-half to one-and-three-quarter inches, not from the crown of the clubhead, but from the top of the face to the bottom. The fairway woods should each drop down in depth about an eighth of an inch.

Generally speaking, the swingers, who tend to hit the ball a little higher, can use a bit less loft; the punchers, who sometimes have problems getting the ball up, use more. And in each of our descending twenty-five yard categories of power, about an eighth of an inch less depth in the driver face should be used.

The length of the face from toe to heel is not nearly so important, since all but an inch on either side of its center is not really usable. Two to two-and-a-half inches is plenty, if you feel it is. Any added surface beyond that would be merely to give you confidence—a factor which, of course, must not be overlooked.

Coming to the irons, the guiding principle is to have them slightly stiffer shafted than the accompanying woods. A light "S" shafted wood then calls for a medium "S" shafted iron, but not an "X." The swing weight should be the same as the woods, or slightly lighter, since the lighter head makes for greater backspin. The grip dimensions should be the same. Personally I favor diamond-shaped grips, but so far I haven't been able to talk anyone into making them. And, incidentally, no grip on a wooden club should be much longer than the width of the player's hands. Such material deadens shaft action appreciably, and shouldn't cover more than it has to. With the irons, especially the short irons, you are jockeying up and down the shaft with your hands more, and so the grips must be longer. But you have no need to shorten the grip on the driver.

The shape and loft of the iron clubs should relate first to control, not power. As to shape, I have long cried in the wilderness for a more curved sole line on irons. I went so far as to advocate the diamond shape here, too, but up to now the only concession I can see is in the rocker-sole line. This curving sole puts that part of the face which is not going to hit the ball up off the ground where there is less chance of it catching the turf and twisting the club in your hands. Especially with the pitching irons this absence of turf grabbing, or gathering, at the heel and toe, is mandatory. Never get a pitching iron with a long straight sole. On these delicate shots it will lead to nothing but frustration, the toe catching one time, the heel the next.

Then too in selecting the wedge, shy away from the big, straight, heavy, bulbous sole line, an inch or an inch-and-a-half wide, which is particularly useless anywhere but in sand, and useless there, too, unless the sand is exceptionally soft with the ball sitting up on top of it. A narrow, curved sole a half inch wide or less, with the front lip inverted ten degrees, makes for a much handier club in the bunker, and it can be used for the short pitches as well.

In the matter of loft, three degrees of difference in the longer irons is about right, but I like a four-degree difference from the seven iron up through the wedge. True, this makes for weaker clubs—a wedge of forty-degree loft, for example. But they have much more playability. You can pinch shots with them as well and still have enough loft. And whenever you need more power you can always go down to the straighter-faced club.

In ladies' clubs the same general rules apply; as well as the same general mistakes. Most ladies now are using shafts that are too whippy and clubs that are too heavy in swing weight. Stiffer-shafted, lighter clubs would help most of them. Though not as stiff shafted as the men's clubs, theirs should not be much different in swing weight. The faces should be shallower, especially in the fairway woods. The driver, as we have said, ought to have twelve degrees of loft, but should be reasonably deep-faced—not less than an inch-and-a-quarter.

As women improve and begin to step up their power, which they're doing all the time (you cannot call Mickey Wright a light hitter, for instance, by any standard but that of the top touring male pros), they should go through the same equipment adjustments as we have suggested for men.

Whenever you need to change clubs, a good set of used ones is really a better purchase than a cheap new set. The latter usually offers you only one type of shaft and you must be very lucky for that shaft to fit you. Good second-hand clubs can be chosen to conform more closely to your particular needs.

As to the actual material now used in wood clubs, the old standby, persimmon, is still all right. But it seems to be losing some ground. These trees have been cut over so many times that good grades of persimmon are much harder to obtain now. The more porous, peeling, inferior grade, must be filled with lead, which reduces shock up to a point. But past that point it makes the clubhead break or splinter more easily. Persimmon also needs an insert; the Teflon that I am experimenting with now seems to be the best once you arrive at the right thickness.

Lately laminated woods have been substituted more and more for persimmon. But their virtues are unluckily against them. They absorb so little moisture that they resist stains or attractive finishes. And they are so hard that they tend to break manufacturers' tools. As a result they are avoided, though not for any good fundamental reason. On the contrary they are excellent in all important aspects. The new plastics offer longer-lasting possibilities, too, such as permanently-colored clubheads all the way through. They are impervious to moisture and even to rust.

But it is in putting equipment that the golf nut really has his field day. Our La Jolla shop carries about a hundred putters (on display all the time) and they are constantly being taken out and sampled by everyone. A player will trade his in and buy a used one from us that in turn was traded in by a friend of his last week. The height of these complications was finally reached when one of our club's best putters, who was constantly changing clubs and experimenting, came to my assistant and complained about the disparity between two prices of the very same design of putter. "Look at this one, costing so and so," he said; "and then look at that one, it's so much cheaper." "Yes," my assistant said. "The first one is new; the second one used to be yours. You traded it to us last month."

I myself prefer a putter with a moderately stiff shaft. I hear people say, "I get a much finer feel of distance with the softer shaft." But I have more confidence in club experts like Admiral Brandon whose opinion, in this case, happens to reinforce my own. He says that in finding exactly the right shaft stiffness for any particular head weight of any particular putter (or to put it the other way around: the right weight for the particular shaft), you should first get a head heavy enough to feel as you waggle the putter gently back and forth. Then, he advises, you should start taking weight out of it down to that point where, making the same gentle waggle, you stop feeling the weight, or "give" in the shaft. Now you have the right balance between head weight and shaft stiffness. Stiffer shafts thus need more head weight, softer ones less.

Let me add my own conviction that a putter should either be light or heavy, not medium, and that the face should not be too lively. Aluminum with a little lead in it produces the right sort of dead hit, and there are other materials which qualify, including a line of glass-faced putters of my own design.

The primary requirement, however, is still to have the right degree of loft on the putter-face. If you play the ball back toward the right foot, or lean your hands prominently forward ahead of the club—and I disapprove of both these methods—you compound the problems. But if you play the ball in the correct position, the loft on the putter face should be proportional to its depth, or normally about three-and-a-half or four degrees.

A deeper-faced putter, such as the Schenectady made famous by Walter Travis, needs more loft than that. Similarly, a very shallow-faced blade needs less.

Too much loft makes the ball pitch a bit as it leaves the club;

this affects the accuracy of its roll. But too little loft is much worse. Except on very smooth greens a putter too straight-faced drives the ball down into the nap, or grain, and makes it bounce.

The Cash-In or Bull's Eye blade putters seem to be among the soundest made today, as their sales fortunately bear out. And they have several special features which are important. The two straight lines, on front and back, give you your best chance to line up the blade square to the hole. The near center, or semi-center shaft also makes for delicate balance. Further, it indicates more exactly where the ball should be hit—*just next to the shaft*—and eliminates most of the possible torsion from that hit.

I myself still use a mallet-head putter, but mainly because I have used one since childhood. I guess I just can't break the habit. Among the leading putters the choice between blade and mallet is about equal. Horton Smith used both. Bobby Jones, Jerry Barber, Johnny Revolta are exponents of the blade. Travis and Casper of the mallet.

You still have choices, of course, in how you assemble all your clubs—in what to put in and what to leave out of your set. So long as my requests for a set of six woods, six irons, a wedge and a putter get no response from the manufacturers (and I don't recommend such a set for the better player, anyway), the best assembly for the average man is probably five woods, seven irons, a wedge and a putter. I favor five woods over four, or less, for all but the very strongest players. Yet the recent advent of the 1½, 2½, 3½ and 4½ woods gives us more leeway in selection. These special clubs are an attempt to span the five woods with four so that the player can add a pitching wedge, or a two iron, or a jigger or some other club which suits his particular needs. I favor these innovations. They widen the area of choice. I don't use them myself because I've found a double-duty wedge that suits me. I can then carry the five woods. It's that simple. But look into these various combinations and see if they free you to add some other club which you would like to have in your bag.

If a person wants to start on a more modest scale, with a skeleton set of clubs that will get him going without bankrupting him right off the bat, I suggest for his wooden clubs a driver and a four wood. If he's in the absolute beginner class, he might substitute the two wood for the driver and use it for double duty. But I like the 1-4 combination better than the 1-3 or 2-3. Then in the irons he could skip every other club and buy 3-5-7-9 and putter, or leave out the three iron and add the wedge.

Finally, I should help you choose from the raft of golf balls now offered, especially since they, too, seem costly these days. When it comes to picking them I warn you to stay away from the off-brand lines. Some of the worst junk comes from these sources. With nearly solid centers, and just enough strands of rubber added to justify calling them Haskell-centered, many of them are good only for driving ranges. I prefer cut or damaged good balls to them. Some manufacturers put out a few properly-made balls to advertise a new name, and then lower the grade of the balls. This is nothing short of fraud.

With the top-grade balls, on the other hand, it is not a matter of quality, or of pitting one against the other, so much as matching your individual capability to their different performance purposes. It won't make you hit farther, for example, to use the Titleist 100 or the Wilson Staff simply because you hear George Bayer does. (Actually I don't even know that he does, so don't sue me one way or the other.)

For the best high-quality ball in the world may still not be wound properly for the kind of blow you give it. A great deal of misinformation gets passed around about compressions. In my own case, I need a medium to medium-high range (since compared to the average golfer, I hit the ball a bit harder and a bit farther). But I am not at all positive about how the major manufacturers designate them. There is much talk about the hundred-plus compression—supposedly incorporated in a couple of products that I learned through trial and error are not effective for me. Even in comparatively warm weather, when resilience is influenced to a degree, they sound and feel like rocks when I hit them, and they go nowhere.

EQUIPMENT

At the other end of the scale, when I hit a Spalding Kro-Flite, or its equivalent in other lines (like the Dunlop Green or Titleist Red, and I'm not going to try to name them all), this sixty-five to seventy compression feels too soft and mushy on my club. It still however, goes better than the ball wound with maximum tightness, and the looser winding makes it far more durable and "cut-resistant." But it also leaves something to be desired in click and feel, and it is a little too lively on the greens.

With the Spalding Dot, or the normal top-grade Titleist, the Royal, or Max-fli Red, or any other average-to-high compression ball, perhaps between seventy-five and ninety, I feel admirably suited.

Power divisions such as we set up earlier, in twenty-five yard segments, are good guides here in larger units. The 225-260 hitter can use the top-flight balls, though I question whether any but the very peak of that group can use the hundred-plus. The 175-225 group will suffer only at the very top, if at all, with a more loosely wound ball. Below 175 yards these low-compression balls are called for without question. And when it comes to the lighter-hitting lady, the Spalding Kro-Flite, Dunlop Green, Titleist Red or Royal Queen fills the bill.

At any rate, modern balls are a far cry from those I remember when I first started to play golf. The Haskell center, and the skin-tight, one-piece, Cadwell-Geer patented cover give us a standardized product now. The USGA and the Royal and Ancient keep manufacturers from adding to the velocity attainable. Muzzle tests now flash a red light whenever a ball comes out too fast. So uniformity has become the keynote.

But my memory goes back to Pinehurst and the North-South Open of 1930, where I was playing with a rather make-shift set of clubs and a ball called (not very aggressively or positively) the Wilson Why-not. I was finishing the third round in the sole company of two totally unknown amateurs. One of them, having shot in the neighborhood of a hundred, offered to withdraw to keep from damaging my chances of accomplishing something in the tournament on the last eighteen holes still to be played that afternoon. As I was eating lunch just before going out again, Johnny Dawson, then a Spalding representative, gave me a half dozen Spalding Dots to use. These were the first Dots I had ever seen, much less hit, and I was delighted (they measured in pennyweights those days, fifty, forty, thirty, and it made for a clearer set of distinctions than we now have).

The gift was not exactly charity on Johnny's part, since the scoreboard showed me very near the lead as I went back out on the course. I was exhilarated, anyway, by this rarified air around first place. But in the reduced company of one amateur, and galleried only by Dawson, I began to hit shots I had never hit before in my life. Starting off the last nine, Johnny found out that Armour had fallen by the wayside, and that Walsh was not doing any better. I looked certain to be in front or tied. Needing a good back nine to win, I made a thirty-three, on that fine, testing course.

On the last hole, in the first two rounds I had plugged a two wood deep into the bank of a trap about twenty yards in front of the green, from where I struggled to one seven and one five. But now in my sudden euphoria I reached the green with a four-iron second shot and made a good four. I was never to reach it again, either, with so short a club, in all the times I went back there.

It was my first major victory, coming when I was dead broke, and on my way East to take a position with Craig Wood at the Forest Hills Field Club. The runner-up, Frank Walsh, sent Craig a wire that night: "Congratulations. After this keep unknown assistants at home." And I sent a telegram of my own back to Arkansas, addressed to the future Mrs. Runyan: "Joan, I won." Come to think of it, I wonder if they've got any of those Spalding Dots left?

CHAPTER 16

TOURNAMENT TIPS

I really don't know why, in a chapter of tournament tips, I use the plural at all. Ultimately they all boil down to one the Boy Scouts used first: Be Prepared. Your performance under the stress of tournament play may seem to you to allow almost any outcome, if you keep your head about you. You tell yourself if you do this right or that right, or have a little luck, you will win, and that the issue is all before you.

But that's not so. It's the difference between a battle and a war. The latter is really decided by long-range factors that can't be seen in any individual contest, no matter how it comes out. So in golf how you function in tournaments, where everyone sees the result, is determined largely by what preparations you make beforehand.

I mean preparations of every kind. Mental and physical. And I don't restrict them, either, to name tournaments whose results turn up in the important papers. There's no may to measure inner desire. For I'm sure the match played by a high handicapper who has never won a tournament but has suddenly improved to become a finalist in the President's Cup or Club Championship, puts him under as much tension and stress (not unpleasantly: since he's out there for the stimulation of competition) as the Open does to the major professionals. To keep from letting himself down, he, too, has to know something about getting ready for a tournament.

Now when I was a fledgeling on my first Western tour, so hungry for bits and pieces of prize money that I could almost taste it, I wore myself out trying to get rested up. I'd eat an early dinner, with no friends around for company or talk which might have relaxed me after that day's play. Afterwards, I'd hurry to bed around eight o'clock to really sleep hard, I'd tell myself. So I'd roll and toss all night. Next morning I'd not be much better off. And I'd go back out to the golf course so tired I couldn't wiggle.

Of course I have learned a lot since those days. The press of endless professional duties around a country club—and again, it's what I'm there for: I like them—certainly does have an adverse effect on the fine edge of competitive golf as it's played today. Yet no matter how worn down I get, if I go off by myself for just four or five days to get ready for some event I'd particularly like to do well in, I soon feel all the old pulses begin to beat right again. And it isn't long before this shows up on the golf course, too. I've made these periodic stands in the past, especially in 1938, when I'd all but disappeared from contention in the major tournaments. And it resulted in the victory over Snead, which is still remembered more than anything else I've ever done.

I still repeat the process whenever I want to get myself ready for an important event. It is more intensive than I would advise the non-professional to undertake. But by cutting down proportionately on his program the average golfer can also prepare himself better for particular tournaments. For the total amount of time spent is not so important as the distribution of that time.

My own regimen consists of getting up early and eating a good meal, really the most important thing of all for anyone doing much physical exercise. If it's the day of the tournament, I want to get this meal over with at least an hour ahead of time, to let the body complete its functions before I get out on the course, and to give me time to practice leisurely. What particular food or diet is best I'll leave to the nutritionists, except to add one prejudice of my own, which I feel my experience corroborates.

If there is a miracle food, it is not the widely-touted gelatins or anything else, but *honey*. I put it on toast or bread at breakfast, and I even carry it with me in my golf bag. Taking a nip of it now and then keeps me from getting hungry and also seems to have a calming effect on the nerves. I know this therapy may be all in my mind, but I believe in it. So I pass it on for whatever it's worth.

I avoid stimulants of all kinds, except cambric tea occasionally. I do not smoke. This helps me get back into shape quickly when I start my training program. Actually, it seems to me that smoking probably has a worse effect in cutting down a player's stamina than moderate drinking does.

To guard against leg cramps—which can ruin you in a tournament—a quart of milk a day is recommended, if it doesn't make you too fat. If it does, quinine pills will see you through. But take them two days before the tournament. They are likely to have some effect on vision the day after they are used.

After getting my meal of the right foods at the right time, the order of practice itself is important. You should always practice the full shots last, just before you go to the tee; to hit a full shot there, of course.

Lengthy practice putting before you go out for a round can have the opposite effect you want. It may tighten you up again, especially if you're not as young as you used to be. I do the putting and chipping first, out by the practice green, and not necessarily toward any particular hole there. I may just lay the practice bag somewhere and putt and chip at it. My objective is simply to get the rhythm going, to find my feel of distance. And to do so I want a pile of balls, not just two or three. Then I can stand in one place and hit them until I get the stroke I want, without having to break off and go after them just when I might be developing the proper feel.

I also hit a few bunker shots, not to acquire the technique, since I've got it down pretty pat by now, but to get a sense of proper distance from the sand. My entire greenside session will consume from a half-hour to forty-five minutes. But if you decide on a total practice time of a half-hour, for example, you should certainly give the first ten minutes of it to getting the feel of the chips and putts.

Then I'll go to the practice tee, start hitting pitch shots and working through the bag of clubs by skipping perhaps every other one. If this is not a tournament day, I may continue for a little over an hour here, making a total of two practice hours in all. If a tournament match is scheduled, however, I cut down on the time devoted to the full shots, keeping to a total of an hour, or an hour-and-a-quarter at the very most. However, I never cut down at all on chipping and putting.

After two hours of practice, on non-playing days, I'll get some lunch and some rest. For I am sure that as we grow older, even though we need less *sleep*, we need more *rest*, and two practice periods a day are better than one. It's hard to find the time, but the two intervals—even if the mid-day rest is only a half-hour—make a world of difference for me.

Following the rest period after lunch, I repeat the morning's practice session with exactly the same routine. Two more hours there does me infinitely more good than going out on the course to play, unless I am totally unfamiliar with the layout. When this second practice period is completed I take a shower, relax with some friends, eat my dinner with Joan and perhaps play a little gin or bridge (not for high stakes, though, and I don't want to gamble heavily on the course either, since it uses up the very nerves I need to rest). At any rate, by the week's end, I've got no excuses.

And I think some such program, in smaller doses, will work wonders for anyone. Two separate sessions—of a half-hour apiece—will probably do more actual good, in improving your method of striking the ball—than eighteen holes of play.

Now, and only now, we are ready to talk about positive thinking. It is true that even with this thorough preparation behind me, I may go out in the tournament and act like a mental underdog. Certainly I still have to put into practice all the important tenets of good psychology. I mustn't fuss and fume at myself when things go wrong, or break into a nervous half-run, half-walk trying to get the whole bad business over with when trouble does arise. If there is a hazard to one side, I mustn't tell myself not to hit the ball there, but must turn that advice around and concentrate on where I *am* trying to hit it.

We have covered these governing inner directives in another chapter, and I certainly believe in their importance. I am only trying to say here that, without a background of thorough preparation, it is not even fair to cite these psychological hints. Without careful practice they are merely whistling in the dark.

It is also best not to push these inner directives too far. The ninety golfer playing in a tournament should not crank himself up mentally to believe he can shoot par. His performance is then less likely to come up to his usual standard. Nobody is suddenly going to become a scratch player in a tournament. Your play there will reflect your play in practice beforehand.

If you are currently a bogey golfer, you should plan your round like one for this particular tournament. You should aim second shots where you have the best chance to get on the green in three, to make sure of fives and to set up possibilities of fours here and there. Finally, the most reliable tension-solver, which applies up and down the range of golfing ability, is to convince yourself that whatever jitteriness you feel is liberally shared by others. They are under the same guns, so they are going to make similar mistakes. You should believe that you can make mistakes, without ruining yourself. And by telling yourself this, you are much less likely to make them.

In conclusion, I hope you will forgive any fanatic sound this book may have. I was from the beginning, am now, and ever will be an enthusiast of this game. It has been so infinitely rewarding to me, in experiences I have had, people I have met and places I have been that I can never adequately repay it. Still, I hope this book can apply as at least one installment on that debt. And if I have set down anything here that helps you to get a fraction of my enjoyment from this sport, I'll feel very happy. With that, I have only these last words. *Get at it.*